Praise for *Get Quiet*

"With its stories, methods, and embraceable guidance, Get Quiet provides a timely antidote to the overwhelm that so many of us are feeling. Just as healthy foods are the right medicine for your body, Get Quiet is the right medicine for your soul."

— **Mark Hyman, M.D.**, author of the
#1 *New York Times* bestseller *Young Forever*

"In a noisy world full of distraction, Get Quiet by Elaine Glass is a much-needed source of wisdom. Elaine's personal and professional insights offer both inspiration and guidance so we can step away from the ceaseless hustle of modern life. Chapter by chapter, the book's compelling prose illuminates a path for hearing our inner voice—a source that empowers, strengthens, and connects us to our true purpose. Get Quiet offers readers a journey to the heart of what matters."

— **BJ Fogg, Ph.D.**, behavior scientist, Stanford University,
and *New York Times* best-selling author of *Tiny Habits*

"Disruptions begone. If you've been looking for a way to unclutter your mind, this book is it. Elaine and her 'Get Quiet' wisdom will wake you up to a world more beautiful. It's a must-read."

— **Vani Hari**, *New York Times* best-selling author
and founder of Food Babe and Truvani

"In our fast-paced world of exponential technology, Elaine Glass elegantly invites us to harness the power of profound quiet, creating a regulated nervous system that has the capacity to quickly transition our energy from stuck to authentically flowing again."

— **Mastin Kipp**, 2x best-selling author and creator
of Functional Life Coaching™

"With deep insight and inspiration, this book has the power to connect you with your soul and transform your life. Elaine Glass gives us what the world desperately needs— to understand the gift of getting quiet and slowing down by providing a profound tool and process to do it!"

— **Kristen Butler**, founder of Power of Positivity and author of *The Comfort Zone*

"With a voice that is strong yet gentle, Elaine Glass transports you to a serene and profound inner space as she walks you into your very own labyrinth. You get to access your source of energy through the miraculous Get Quiet Way. You are at long last removed from the noise around you and are suddenly feeling attuned and healed from all the burdens your body, heart, and mind carried for so long."

— **Christina Rasmussen**, author of *Second Firsts*, *Where Did You Go?*, and *Invisible Loss*

"In a world chock-full of distraction, clutter, and noise, we are so often told to embrace the silence. And now, a practical blueprint finally exists that teaches you in an easy-to-understand way how to actually 'Get Quiet.' If you live in the modern world, Elaine Glass's book is a must-read."

— **Ben Greenfield**, founder of KION

"Get Quiet came at the perfect time for me; and I felt like Elaine had written directly to me as I read her words. Her message is so needed and so helpful in today's world; and it helped me reconnect and open my heart in a way that I hadn't gotten to feel in years. I know that you will find peace in Get Quiet as well. Spend time reading it and practicing the meditations in your life!"

— **Katie Wells**, Wellness Mama

GET
QUIET

GET
QUIET

7 SIMPLE PATHS TO THE
TRUTH OF WHO YOU ARE

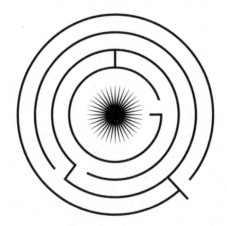

ELAINE GLASS

HAY HOUSE LLC
Carlsbad, California • New York City
London • Sydney • New Delhi

Copyright © 2024 by Elaine Glass

Published in the United States by: Hay House LLC: www.hayhouse.com®
Published in Australia by: Hay House Australia Pty. Ltd.: www.hayhouse.com.au
Published in the United Kingdom by: Hay House UK, Ltd.: www.hayhouse.co.uk
Published in India by: Hay House Publishers India: www.hayhouse.co.in

Cover design: Micah Kandros
Interior design: Julie Davison

The author of this book does not dispense medical advice or prescribe the use of any technique as a form of treatment for physical, emotional, or medical problems without the advice of a physician, either directly or indirectly. The intent of the author is only to offer information of a general nature to help you in your quest for emotional, physical, and spiritual well-being. In the event you use any of the information in this book for yourself, the author and the publisher assume no responsibility for your actions.

**Cataloging-in Publication Data is on
file at the Library of Congress**

Tradepaper ISBN: 978-1-4019-7626-2
E-book ISBN: 978-1-4019-7627-9
Audiobook ISBN: 978-1-4019-7628-6

10 9 8 7 6 5 4 3 2 1
1st edition, April 2024

Printed in the United States of America

This product uses responsibly sourced papers and/or recycled materials. For more information, see www.hayhouse.com.

To Matthew and Mike and the

infinite love that unites us

CONTENTS

Step In xiii

PART I: Beginning

Chapter One: Get Quiet 5

Chapter Two: The Labyrinth 23

PART II: Healing

Chapter Three: Get Living...39

Chapter Four: Get Energized.. 61

Chapter Five: Get Present...85

Chapter Six: Get Rest.. 101

PART III: Discovering

Chapter Seven: Get Grounded.. 121

Chapter Eight: Get Excited...135

Chapter Nine: Get Inspired 151

Chapter Ten: Get Connected 167

Conclusion: Living a Quiet Life... 175

Discover More... 179

Acknowledgments 181

About the Author..183

The rush and pressure of modern life are a form,
perhaps the most common form, of its innate violence.
To allow oneself to be carried away by a multitude
of conflicting concerns, to surrender to too many
demands, to commit oneself to too many projects,
to want to help everyone in everything, is to succumb to
violence. The frenzy of our activism neutralizes our work
for peace. It destroys our own inner capacity for peace.
It destroys the fruitfulness of our own work, because it
kills the root of inner wisdom which makes work fruitful.

— THOMAS MERTON,
CONJECTURES OF A GUILTY BYSTANDER

STEP IN

As you step into the labyrinth, you can't help but notice how quiet it is. You can hear birds chirping and singing nearby, their chorus interrupted only by the sound of gravel crunching under your feet. Your ability to hear, to almost absorb these sounds feels somehow heightened, as if you have dropped into a whole new level of listening.

You feel a rush of comforting energy as you take that first step onto the circling path in front of you. This new energy seems to remain constantly at your side as you continue into the labyrinth, like it's walking alongside you. Your curiosity is piqued by the distinct feeling that you're not alone here, that you're surrounded by energy that is deeply loving and supportive, while also playful and light.

The paths of the labyrinth pull you deeper into that silence, and you become aware of yourself in a way that you're usually not. You're present for the way your body slightly shifts as you walk, the gentle rhythmic beating of your heart, the way thoughts float through your mind, the sway of your hips, the strength of your legs moving you forward, and your feet treading the ground slowly and intentionally. It feels as if everything about you is settling here: your body, heart, mind, and soul. With this, your attention shifts away from the stresses of daily life that weighed heavy on your shoulders when you arrived.

And then you reach the center of the labyrinth. There, waiting for you, is the glowing ball of all that divine power you came into the world with. You recognize it at once, even though you've forgotten about it for all these years. Despite everything you've been through, all the responsibility and noise you feel weighing down upon you in day-to-day life, that ball of power is still so pristine and untouched. Suddenly you understand that it's been there all this time, so accessible, just waiting to reveal itself to you so that you can remember.

PART I

BEGINNING

WHEN WAS THE LAST TIME

YOU WERE QUIET ENOUGH TO

HEAR YOUR SOUL'S VOICE?

WHEN WAS THE LAST

TIME YOU HEARD THE

GUIDING AND SUPPORTIVE

MESSAGES THAT YOUR

INTUITION AND THE

UNIVERSE ARE SENDING YOU?

CHAPTER ONE

GET QUIET

The only way you will ever awaken is through silence, not through analyzation of facts. Not by sorting out good and bad, but through simple silence, letting go. Letting go of all thoughts, all the hurts, all the dogmas and concepts. Letting go of these things daily.

— ROBERT ADAMS, *SILENCE OF THE HEART*

Quiet is our natural state, but that can be hard to believe on a moment-to-moment basis as we race through the day taking care of our family, our job, and our daily tasks, filling our precious spare moments with text messages, social media, or an endless scroll. Ask yourself: When was the last time you were quiet enough to hear your soul's voice? When you were not just in a quiet place, but in a quiet state where your body, heart, and mind were so harmonious and at peace that you could easily and freely connect with your soul? When was the last time you heard the guiding and supportive messages that your intuition and the universe are sending you? Perhaps in earlier times, when the world was slower and existed in a more pristine and natural state, it was easier to hear the guidance that's available to each of us. But, as I'm sure you already know, that's not the case anymore—especially for women. I'm guessing it's been a long time since you've had this experience of true, profound *quiet*. And if you have, it was likely a fleeting moment or in a situation where you were removed from your day-to-day life and environment.

Today women can do anything, which often means that we end up doing *everything*, nurturing everyone around us, unnecessarily carrying the weight of the world, stretching ourselves so thin that there's no room left for quiet, no room for ourselves. The days go by too quickly, and the nights are spent tossing and turning, worrying about what wasn't done and already thinking ahead to tomorrow. The cost of this is much higher than just exhaustion, which is bad enough. Women are more burned out, depressed, and anxious than ever before. We've lost touch with our femininity, creativity, and natural flow, which means we've lost our inner connection, our sense of purpose, and our very selves. It's a noisy way to live. Novelist Anne Morrow Lindbergh expresses this perfectly in her book *Gift from the Sea* when she writes, "This is not the life of simplicity but the life of multiplicity that the wise men warn us of. It leads not to unification but to fragmentation. It does not bring grace, it destroys the soul. And this is not only true of my life, I am forced to conclude, it is the life of millions of women in America."

The most rebellious and counter-culture thing you can possibly do today is to get quiet, yet quiet is an essential state to be in to live a life that you love, in a body you're comfortable in, with a peaceful mind, heart, and soul. This quiet is essential to finding yourself again, to getting unstuck in all of the places where life currently feels stagnant. In this book, not only are you going to find out what quiet—true, deep, profound quiet—feels like, but you're also going to learn how to stay grounded in it.

Make no mistake: establishing and preserving a sense of quiet in your life and in your being is one of the most important things you will ever do. For yourself, for your family and loved ones, and for the world at large, for that matter. When you're quiet in this way, you can truly *hear*. You can hear the whispers of the universe guiding you toward your life's purpose and all of those things that are meant for you. You can become attuned to all of the spiritual support that has been here all along, trying to catch your attention. And all of this will allow you to bring your unique purpose to this world that needs it so much. For many women, this might feel selfish and even scary. After all, we're taught to give and nurture, not to take up space. As you rewrite this programming, remember the words of the late, great musician Leonard Cohen: "It isn't about turning your back on the world; it's about stepping away now and then so that you can see the world more clearly and love it more deeply."

You were, quite literally, born for this.

This book is all about moving energy and then getting quiet enough to hear what that energy is telling you. When you are living amid stagnancy and noise, unable to hear yourself and the universe around you, it's impossible to live the life that you truly desire—the life that is rightfully yours. When this is the case, even if you create the life you think you want, you'll likely find that it's unsatisfying because you built it based on a vision that was polluted by noise—the noise of the world, the noise in your head, in your life. All of this noise mutes those far more quiet, wiser, and more true voices. *Those* are the voices that will ultimately lead you in the direction your soul desires. And they are difficult to hear in this modern world of ours, particularly for women who have so much to balance and juggle, so many competing voices in their lives, all of which demand to be heard.

When you can't hear this important information, you end up building a life based on the past because, of course, that's your greatest measure. In other words, you're building either on stagnant energy or on very surface-level dreams and desires because they're easy to observe; you're building your life off goals and to-do lists rather than from your heart's attunement to your most true longings. When this is the case, your life and your future are built on stuck energy. As a life coach and spiritual guide for more than a decade, I see this play out in my clients' lives all of the time—to the extent that I can clearly see a pattern: we work and work toward something, and then when we finally get it, we come to find that we don't even want it after all. This can feel confusing—and certainly disappointing—but it makes sense if you think about it from this perspective of noise and stuck energy.

7

Emotion is energy, so if you're not processing it and moving it through you, that means it's stuck. Stuck inside of you, keeping you closed off, in the past, and unable to hear and sense what is meant for you. It's extremely difficult to find your way from this point. You're not meant to live like this, because the things that you want want you just as much. They will talk to you if only you can clear the way for them to get through, and then become quiet and present enough to hear them. The messages are everywhere. Once you are awake enough to recognize them, life becomes a thrilling, deeply gratifying, and even magical experience.

Once the valve has been released and the energy is flowing, suddenly these messages aren't so difficult to decipher anymore. In fact, you will likely find that when you encounter or stumble upon something—an idea, an activity, a person, a possibility—that really moves you, you can *feel* it from head to toe. Your channels are open, you're not stuck in or holding on to the energy of the past, so instead, there is room for the energy that wants to lead you into the future to make itself known. When you have this experience and are present enough to feel it, you will come to understand that often something wants *you*. And that something will make itself known if only you can tune in to hear it call. It's often quite surprising, because these calls are not coming from your logical mind, from past experiences, or as the result of goals you've built toward. Instead they're just meant for you, even if they don't seem to make sense or follow a linear path.

I can promise that you are being called too. To hear this call, you must do two things. First, you have to move old energy so that new energy can flow through. And second, you must create a clear channel to receive new energy that's meant specifically for you.

Cut through the Noise to Get to the Quiet

In the pages that come, I'm going to share the Get Quiet Way with you, which is a process to heal and shift energy in the key energy centers of the body. This is the same practice that I share with my clients when they're seeking a new sense of vitality, purpose, and joy in their relationships, their work, and their lives in general. I never set out to devise a system; instead I accidentally discovered it in my own healing process—or, rather, I was shown it, but more about that in a bit.

The Get Quiet Way was born more than a decade ago, entirely because of all of the noise and fear in my own life. I couldn't hear myself, let alone the loving guidance of my inner voice or the universe at large. Even though the world was a quieter place then than it is today, with fewer apps to distract me, text messages to respond to, and social media accounts to manage, all of the noise that constantly enveloped me still felt deafening.

But technology is only part of the distraction. Our lives in general are noisy. We are constantly surrounded by a cacophony of noise from all of the different areas of our lives, each battling for our attention 24 hours a day. When we escape the literal noise for those precious hours of sleep and rest, our mind continues to chatter away, and our body and heart often do too. In the midst of all this noise from different corners of our lives and ourselves, the only voices that can turn the volume up high enough to capture our attention are the voices of fear, because fear speaks loudly and prattles on incessantly. It's bound and determined to get our attention . . . and it won't stop until it does.

Meanwhile, the wiser, loving, and supportive voice—your soul's voice—is gentle. It speaks softly, and it is not loud or forceful. Yes, this loving and supportive voice is more powerful, peaceful, wise, and true than the others, but it's also easy to lose in the noise and busy-ness of life.

The noisy and fear-based world we live in promotes conformity and blocks out the truth of who we are and why we're here, so it's up to us to find ways to support ourselves in answering that age-old question: *Who am I?* This is the question you're here to answer in this lifetime because you are who you are for a reason. Until you understand who that is, you can't bring the gifts into the world that you alone are uniquely designed to bring. *You are here to know and embrace who you are and to embody that expression at the highest level.* Not only does the world need you to do so, but living into the truest, deepest version of yourself is also how your soul evolves and expands in the way it's meant to during your time on this planet.

This is more important than ever today because we're living in a time when there's not only more noise than ever before, but also more possibility. We currently have the opportunity to connect to higher states of consciousness, powers of self-healing, and higher dimensions than ever before. Perhaps you've noticed that more and more people are waking up to higher states of consciousness. Some have been forced to because of a health scare, the loss of a loved one, a relationship or career issue, or other significant challenges in life. Others have been woken up by more mainstream access to and acceptance of practices like meditation, yoga, and self-care, among others. On a more metaphysical level, I also believe that the higher entities are desperately seeking souls on the 3D plane to heal this planet and humankind and step into a 5D reality. But to hear the call and seize this moment, first we have to live in a state in which we're unaffected (or at least not ruled) by all the noise and distraction that are so pervasive. And that's all it is: noise and distraction, whether it presents as fear, busy-ness, overwhelm, or a lack of purpose and direction.

Getting quiet allows you to get healthy in a sick world.

What we're going to talk about in this book isn't a short-term fix but a sustainable solution that will set you on a path toward living a very different, much more fulfilling life than you are today. This isn't about taking a retreat from the noise but, instead, discovering a new way of living, being, and hearing, all built upon a deep and abiding sense of quiet.

If this sounds like a big promise, that's because it is. It's often difficult to recognize noise for the problem it is, but it is the root cause of so many physical, mental, emotional, and spiritual ailments. These ailments are actually just a symptom of all the noise around and within you. I know this is true in my own life, and I've also seen it play out in the lives of my clients. Clients come to me because they're feeling stuck, lost, disconnected from themselves, without purpose or a sense of their true identity. They come to me because it feels as if their lives are falling apart and they're powerless to create the change they want; sometimes they don't even *know* what change they want, they just know that the way things are right now isn't working. They're dealing with a health crisis, job loss, or divorce, or suffering from the painful experiences that have resulted from making bad decisions. No matter how much success they've found, they still feel incomplete, stuck, and unfulfilled. Worst of all, they can't see the way out.

I've learned over time that each of these issues is not actually the issue at all—it's a symptom of the noise. Until we find a way to rise above that noise and hear different voices than the ones that are breaking through right now, it's very difficult—and I might go so far as to say impossible—to alleviate these symptoms in any sort of true and lasting way. The price for allowing this to persist is just too high: what's at stake is this precious, unique life of yours and your ability to live out exactly what you came here to do.

My world was very loud for many years until it finally reached a crescendo when I was in my early 40s. From the outside, it looked like I had a dream life—or, at least, it was certainly the type of life I'd always thought I wanted. I was married to a doctor, lived in a big house, and had a successful career of my own as a dental hygienist, which I was also fortunate enough to be able to step away from so that I could stay home with my two sons when they were young.

And yet I felt overwhelmed, sad, lonely, and unappreciated in my marriage and powerless in life. I wanted to fix my marriage and create a healthy and loving family for my sons, but everything I did to try to make things better didn't seem to make a difference. There were things I loved about my practice as a dental hygienist, but I was also burning out after working with more than 40,000 patients during my nearly 20 years in the field. For a highly sensitive person like me, being around patients who were fearful and often feeling unwell on a daily basis was taxing. I *did* feel like I could offer them comfort (and I enjoyed doing so), but it came at my own expense when I already had little energy on reserve. I was running around all of the time, constantly giving too much while receiving too little. No matter how much I did or how hard I tried, it still didn't feel like I was doing anything right or like I was enough. There was a heaviness around me, as if my body was weighed down to earth with an anchor. I couldn't even begin to imagine how I might fill my sails enough to create a sense of lightness, personal freedom, or forward movement in my life. That heaviness was especially persistent around my chest and lungs—to the point where it felt as if I couldn't breathe. It was becoming increasingly unbearable to hold all of it. The volume of the world and my life was turned up so high that I lived in a constant state of overwhelm. I felt stuck, disconnected from myself, as if I was flailing around in life, trying to make it from one day— and sometimes one moment—to the next. Throughout all of this, I put a lot of pressure on myself to find much-needed solutions, to make things better, to make *myself* feel better, but that pressure only resulted in more pressure, more heaviness, and more noise. What I didn't understand at the time was that I was *making a decision* to hold all of this heaviness rather than choosing to release it. It didn't feel like that at the time, though; instead, it felt like nothing I did moved my life in the direction I wanted it to go or, more importantly, made me feel how I wanted to feel.

I soldiered on for as long as I could until I started to get sick. I was sick in every way—physically, mentally, emotionally, and spiritually. Years of living as I had been manifested as the autoimmune disease Hashimoto's disease (a thyroid condition), which left me feeling fatigued, foggy, and uncomfortable because of the extra weight I put on as a result. Back then I didn't understand how a lot of the things I was feeling and experiencing were interconnected, but I *did* understand that I was sick because of how I felt in my life, because of all of the things I chose to press through, like living every day feeling sick with worry and sadness, fearing for my future, and fearing for my kids' futures and the ways in which I fretted that I might mess their lives up. Once I was diagnosed, I truly understood that something had to change. *What else is going to happen to me if I continue on like this?* I wondered. I was still young and already my life was starting to crumble. After 13 years and many attempts to create a healthy marriage and family life, I decided it was time to make a big change and leave my husband. For so long—too long—I had been walking along this path that I see so many women walk: carrying anger around that was making me sick in every way. Though some of my anger was projected outward, the truth is that most of my anger and disappointment was with myself and with the point I had allowed my marriage to get to. One thing I knew for sure was that my boys deserved a healthy mom.

Leaving the home we had brought my sons to from the hospital and where all of our family's most important memories had taken place was one of the most difficult moments of my life. It was a decision I'd never wanted to make. It felt as if all my dreams were shattering before my very eyes, and I could do nothing to fix this life that I had wanted so badly and invested so much love and energy into. Not to mention the fact that the future seemed so unclear; I had no idea what was coming next. As I took one last teary glimpse at my home before shutting the door, I felt all the pent-up emotion of the last 13 years rise up within me. The countless long days and nights I'd spent taking care of my sons without any emotional or physical support flashed in front of my eyes. My voice quivered as I said, "My work is done here," to the emptiness.

Meeting Myself

My whole way of life completely and instantly changed. Much more than the change in my living situation and relationship status was the fact that my entire identity changed. Ultimately, this created the space I hadn't known I needed to get quiet so that the other changes that I longed for and that had gone unheard for so long could emerge into my life and into the world. Over the course of the next few years, I set out on a journey that eventually led me to getting quiet enough to hear my own soul's voice and the voice of all of the universal helpers guiding me. With that, all of the patterns of negative thought, judgment, lack of self-love, and general sense of disconnection fell away from my life one by one, as if I were a statue emerging from a marble slab.

This process of getting quiet so that I could hear and attune to what I needed has been the most important personal transformation I've ever gone through in my life, but make no mistake: it's also been challenging, because it's meant that so many things that I knew to be true up until that point radically changed. I knew that I was outgrowing my career as a dental hygienist, but I needed the money from my job to support my children, and I didn't know what else I could do professionally. Since it felt like I couldn't change my situation, I instead decided to change my mindset. I started to devour new information, largely about spiritual topics, and found that I couldn't get enough. I'd been deeply curious about world religions and various cultures' perspectives on spirituality since I was 16, but I had disconnected from my spirituality throughout the past few difficult years. Now I really dove in. I had grown up Jewish, so I already had a religious foundation of faith and a strong sense of God, but this new information was exciting to me; it lit me up. I began to consider the fact that God was not only an external energy, but also within me. As I began to think about God inside of me, I began to think about love as an internal presence and source of support rather than only an external one.

More and more, I was feeling intrigued by many different spiritual paths. What was this growing sense of connection and empowerment that I felt, and how could I explain it? In addition to reading books about spirituality, I soon started attending events where the spiritual thinkers of our time were gathering and speaking. At the time, I couldn't make sense of a lot of what they were saying, but I *did* feel that I was surrounded by like-minded people for the first time in a long time. Still, I didn't know how to translate all of this into my day-to-day life, even though it was clear that the way I was living no longer felt right. Though my heart and mind were expanding, the reality was that I was living with great financial uncertainty and didn't have the freedom or flexibility to take a leap into the unknown.

A woman named KC Miller, the founder of Southwest Institute of Healing Arts (lovingly known as SWIHA by its students and faculty), was speaking at one of these events. I felt drawn to the type of coursework she was offering in the healing arts, but there was no way I could actually make the leap myself. At the end of her talk, KC passed a bowl around and asked me and the other 60 participants in the breakout room to write our names on slips of paper and place them in the bowl. She said she would award an entire program of the winner's choice to the person whose name she pulled. It felt like an entire new career was up for offer! I put my name in the bowl and visualized how it would feel to win and what I would do with the prize.

You're probably expecting to hear that KC did, in fact, pull my name out of the bowl. But she surprised the entire room and granted everyone 100 hours toward a SWIHA program of their choice.

At the end of KC's talk, I walked up to the front of the room with tears streaming down my face. "I want to let you know that I'm not going to let this gift go to waste, and I'm going to use it to the highest level I can," I told her. The next week, I began my Master Life Coaching training.

Even though I didn't know exactly how it would work or what it would look like, I made the leap and started my coaching business after completing my intense and life-changing coursework. Coaching made sense to me because it was a sort of catch-all for what I'd always innately done for people. I was a quiet kid but not isolated. My classmates used to get the sense that they could come up to me and talk, and we would go into deep-dive conversations, even at a young age. My senses had only been heightened in all those years I spent side by side with other humans as they reclined in the dental chair in front of me. I could feel into their body and somehow connect the dots to understand what was happening with their health and in their life. Because I didn't have the language for it, and because it was something that came naturally to me, I didn't understand at the time that what I was actually able to connect to was the field of energy around my patients to help facilitate their healing. I took for granted the fact that I innately understood how to be there and hold space for the fear and discomfort of other humans. I somehow intuited what they needed, even if they couldn't always put words to it.

As my coaching business continued to grow, I furthered my range of abilities by diving deeper into my own personal development, attending more conferences, reading dozens upon dozens of books, and applying it all to my vision of creating a transformative life experience for my clients. I learned and adapted new skills into my business so that I could treat each client uniquely, based on what the person next to me uniquely needed, whether it was hands-on healing energy medicine, working through grief and loss, or identifying and shifting habits and behavior. The ultimate goal with my clients is to create an experience through which they can discover more meaning, joy, and fulfillment in their lives. All of this ultimately boils down to the same things: being near someone and feeling their energy, sensing where it's stuck and how that's manifesting in their body and in their life, and feeling into what can be done to shift that stuck flow of energy. It has also given me the ability to intuitively understand when the story a client is telling me—their symptom, so to speak—isn't actually the cause of their discontent. And, more important, what *is*.

But funnily enough, for all the studying I've done and information I've learned, it's my own personal transformation that has turned out to be the most informative and helpful to my clients. And I've come to learn that our real work here—the work to find peace, purpose, and joy—is to get quiet.

Getting Quiet

Either consciously or unconsciously, many people are afraid to get quiet, usually because they equate silence with isolation. But when you experience the kind of quiet I'm talking about in these pages—a quiet mind, heart, and soul—you'll find that you feel a great deal less fear and a lot more of a sense of security. When you ask the higher realms for the answers you're desperate to learn, you'll be able to access them. You'll find that situations that used to seem overwhelming or impenetrable suddenly feel manageable. You'll have access to answers you've sought for so long, a new understanding of the path that's meant for you, and a sense of inner peace and lightness that you perhaps hadn't even dreamed possible.

Once I was able to access this sense of quiet, my entire life changed. It was as if I went from sitting in a dark, cramped closet to twirling around an expansive room with sunlight streaming through the windows. I became more confident, happier, and healthier. My energy grew lighter, brighter, and stronger as I not only acknowledged my trauma and pain, but also moved through and beyond it. Whereas I was once so serious, now there was joy and playfulness, a general lightening-up of my body and spirit. I was able to more easily give and receive love and tapped into a deep well of compassion I didn't even know I had in me. All of this allowed me to more graciously draw the good things that were meant for me my way. It made me more loving and less judgmental. I became a better mother because I started to see my role as inspiring and supporting my children in becoming who they were uniquely meant to be rather than propelling them along a path I or society thought was right for them. I embraced who I was meant to be, and as a result, I found a new, expansive freedom bubbling up. Getting quiet simultaneously returned me to both my ability to connect to my humanity and to my divinity.

It also led me on a journey that I never could have imagined. While I've always been intuitive and aware of other people's energy, it wasn't until I discovered true quiet that I recognized I had the ability to facilitate healing experiences for others using energy medicine or to channel messages from a source outside of myself that I began to think of as my guides. Depending upon where you are right now, this may or may not sound "out there"; it certainly would've sounded out there to me at one point. I'm a practical person, very much distant from the world of "woo-woo."

But what I've come to understand is that ideas I might have once considered weird or even impossible are actually natural occurrences in this vast universe we live in. It's just that most of us have lived in a world that's anything but natural. The truth of the matter is that we're all channeling information all of the time. There are otherworldly energies all around us, constantly sending us information—we just can't receive it because we live in a way that's far removed from our natural state.

You have no idea what your true potential is, but it's there, just waiting for you to get quiet so that it can present itself. In doing so, you're making yourself an open vessel through which information can flow. You're opening up the pathway to leave that chronic sense of stagnancy behind because new information will be able to find its way to you easily and frequently. This new information has the potential to change not only you and those closest to you, but also your life—and even the world! That information wants to make its way into the world, and it wants to enter through you. It's all very exciting.

Clients often come to me saying that they feel stuck, they don't even know who they are anymore, they feel like they *should* be happy but they're not. They're exhausted by the pace of the world and their lives. Even their downtime is stressful, with to-do lists and thoughts that cycle on endless repeat. They're prompted to see me for a variety of reasons—because they feel disempowered or overwhelmed at work, their relationships are failing, they feel generally alone in the world or physically unwell. My clients are much like I once was: wounded healers who give and give to others to heal and support them but struggle to heal themselves. They're wise and innovative women who haven't been given permission to show up to the world in the way they really want to. And what I've found in the decade-plus I've been coaching clients is that, while they come to see me for a variety of reasons, these reasons are almost always just symptoms of a shared root issue: *too much noise*. And being immersed in all of this noise means that we're not fully living.

On a day-to-day basis, it can be tempting to keep pressing through these issues and feelings—after all, that's what we've been taught to do. To keep giving when we have nothing left to give. To keep working long after the point of exhaustion. To nurture at our own expense. And all the while, we're dying inside, moving further and further away from who we truly are. So, to be clear, this kind of quiet is not a luxury; it is deeply and profoundly necessary and some of the most vital work you'll ever do in your life. You are a soul living out a human experience—and that can be thrilling and challenging. Your soul is here for the primary purpose of lovingly guiding you through this life, and if you can't hear that beautiful soul of yours, of course you feel lost.

If you picked up this book because you're suffering, I hope you can hear this: *You are not alone.* You have access to God, the universe, and a whole team of spiritual helpers who can see what you can't and guide you along the path that you are meant to walk. A path of more ease, more peace, and more purpose. You were born to trust the unseen just as much as you trust what you can see, hear, and feel. The problem is that modern life has muted this with all of the noise and pressure and stress and fear. To hear what is constantly being offered to you takes real quiet.

Before long, you'll learn to turn down all of that static by quieting your body, your mind, and your heart. Once you do this, you'll understand beyond a shadow of a doubt that you were put on this earth right here, right now, to embrace this glorious life and live out your soul's purpose. You will remember that you are never, ever alone, even in your darkest moments. You will be infused with a new sense of clarity that cuts through those feelings of being stuck and lost and stressed. Although you might not feel it right now, that power is already right here, buried inside of you. All you have to do is connect with it, and getting quiet will give you the keys to do just that.

The Get Quiet Way was informed by my experience in the labyrinth, an ancient and sacred path that has long been associated with contemplation and divine connection—a journey of the self toward the self, so to speak. Amid the chaos and noise of the world, it is here that you are able to listen closely to the whispers of your *still small voice*. Within its gentle guidance lies the profound wisdom that leads you toward your true purpose and inner peace. Let me introduce you to it.

THE LABYRINTH WILL

REMIND YOU THAT YOU

HAVE ALL THE LOVE,

POWER, UNDERSTANDING,

CONNECTION, AND

EVERYTHING ELSE YOU

NEED TO GROW AND FULFILL

YOUR PURPOSE IN THIS

LIFETIME ENCODED WITHIN

YOU, JUST WAITING FOR

YOU TO TAP INTO IT.

CHAPTER TWO

THE LABYRINTH

The Paths to Getting Quiet

*The most significant talent is the ability to
penetrate to the depths of our own being.*

— ABRAHAM ISAAC KOOK, RABBI

On the day I first entered the labyrinth more than a decade ago, I stopped at a local café to grab a cup of coffee. I paid for my order and then moved to the other end of the counter to wait for my drink. As I was waiting, I glanced up at the T-shirts displayed on the wall behind the counter, each of which had an old-school library card dangling from it to display the price. A man stepped up next to me and gestured at the cards, then smiled and nodded in approval.

"I know!" I replied. "Aren't they cool?"

As we waited for our orders to come up, this gentleman and I fell into conversation. Although I had plenty of things to do, I had the strong sense that I shouldn't rush away. I somehow knew that I needed to be present for this interaction.

"Do you want to sit down?" he asked me, gesturing to a nearby table.

I nodded, and we each took a seat and immediately fell into a comfortable conversation about this and that. He shared with me that he was in addiction recovery and always seeking out ways to maintain his peace and inner connection. Among the ways he did this, he said, was walking a labyrinth at a place called the Franciscan Renewal Center. I'd heard of labyrinths before but didn't understand exactly what they were. He explained that they're an ancient intricate network of connecting circular pathways that ultimately lead to the center and then back out again. "Kind of like a walking meditation," he said. He told me he thought I might enjoy the experience of walking the labyrinth too.

I was intrigued. By this point I had been a single mom for five years and was beginning to seriously contemplate leaving my career as a dental hygienist in favor of something more aligned with where I was now. I'd spent the last few years seeking and searching, open to anything and everything that might alleviate the pain of long-held grief, sadness, disappointment, and a general sense of uncertainty. After my conversation with the gentleman in the café, I found myself driving to the retreat center, which, as it turned out, was just a half mile away from my house. Although the property was right off a busy road, the labyrinth was tucked away down a long driveway, in the desert that backed up to the center. It felt so removed, as though it might as well be on another planet, far away from the noise and stress of my own life. As I got out of the car and took it all in, I marveled at how I'd spent all of these years living so close and yet completely oblivious to the fact the labyrinth even existed.

I paused at the mouth of the labyrinth and read the small plaque that described what it was and the impact of walking it. I was particularly struck by this part:

> [The labyrinth] can represent the experiences of your own life which have led you to spiritual depth no matter what your faith background may be. The labyrinth often was experienced in place of visiting the Holy Land and other sacred places. Since the labyrinth has been compared to a spiritual pilgrimage, walking the path to the center can be related to that experience. Walking the path from the entrance to the center could also be seen as a symbolic depiction of the soul's journey through life to God.

I took a deep inhale and then stepped into the labyrinth. As I walked, I happily soaked in the quiet and felt the wind brush up against my cheeks and the soft autumn sun on my legs. At an earlier point in my life, I might have felt a little bit crazy walking in circles in the desert, but I was now in a place where I would happily try anything that might help me feel a sense of peace. And thank goodness I was open, because on that first walk around the labyrinth I heard God's voice, clear as day. *Surrender as if you were a duck curled into itself,* the voice said to me. *We can all learn something from that small and vulnerable creature.* And so, as I continued walking the circular paths of the labyrinth, I focused my prayers on surrendering the need to control everything and everyone around me based on my fear of the unknown future. When I returned to my car, I flipped on the radio right at the point where an announcer was saying, "God is with you. Surrender." That *couldn't* be a coincidence . . . right?

Surrendering wasn't something I was exactly primed to do at that point in my life; in fact, I spent a lot of energy holding on for dear life. Nonetheless, I tried to do it anyway because it felt clear to me that the universe was letting me know this was the first step I had to take: to surrender. Obviously, it wasn't something I was able to do overnight, but the message felt important and clear enough that I was able to hold on to it like a talisman as a reminder to practice surrendering on a moment-to-moment basis. It's not like I suddenly didn't worry about how my kids would fare out in the world, if I would ever find love again, or if I would ever be able to financially support my family doing something I was passionate about. But when those thoughts and worries did creep in, I reminded myself that I could surrender them to the divine. With that came a huge and very novel shift in perception.

That first experience in the labyrinth and the impact it had on me was so real and so profound that I didn't return again for another month. It was as if I sensed I had to be ready for this inner journey that I was about to embark on and to be prepared to make the commitment necessary to bring all of the good it had to offer into my life and into the world. I spent the next month mustering .

up the courage to be open to what I could sense I was about to learn. I had the distinct understanding that things were about to change, and I didn't love change at that point in life because it was beyond my control. Only once I felt prepared to release my grip a little bit did I go back to the labyrinth once again. And once again, I felt immediately engulfed by that sense of peace and connection to something far greater than myself. This time the message I heard was: *You are not alone.* I smiled and started singing Michael Jackson's song of the same name as I continued walking through the labyrinth. I bet you can guess what song was playing on the radio when I returned to the car and started the ignition.

After that second walk, I was officially hooked. Walking along the paths of the labyrinth became an important part of my life, and I returned to it at least twice a week for the next several years. I was craving guidance and feeling desperate for answers to all of the difficult questions that had piled up in my life. Looking back, I see that version of myself almost as a baby, just learning about the world around me and reliant upon wiser and more experienced guides to help me take those first tentative steps. Almost every time I went to the labyrinth, I heard a clear answer to whatever question was playing on my mind or settled in my heart or soul that day. The answers were succinct and clear, and I could feel them land throughout my entire body. They felt completely different from the thoughts that usually raced through my mind and nervous system. I believe that the reason I was able to receive these messages so consistently and hear them so clearly is because walking the labyrinth put me in a state of relaxation, no matter what else was going on in my life at the time. There was something about being there that settled my body, mind, and soul in a deeper way than I'd ever experienced before. In this restful state, I could hear my soul's voice—really, for the first time ever.

I craved my visits to the labyrinth, almost like I was reuniting with a long-lost lover, and before long, my walks fell into a consistent pattern. I began along the first path by feeling into and quieting the energy in my body, focusing on my abdomen as I walked. Then, as I emerged on the second path, my attention was called to my heart, to actually feeling what was there rather than blocking it as I had become so accustomed to doing. The third path called me to quiet my busy mind; the fourth path, to unravel the stored-up tension in my hips by relaxing and learning to receive; the fifth, to simultaneously use my feet to ground down to the earth and channel heavenly support. On the sixth path, I was able to visualize my legs moving me toward my purpose, then connect with intuitive messages that I came to understand moved me ever closer to my dreams on the seventh path. At the center of the labyrinth, I stood in silence and soaked in the blissful feeling of wholeness and connection to everything within and around me.

Without fail, every time I left the labyrinth, the message that had been offered to me as I walked would repeat itself as I left, whether it was through a song playing on the radio, a billboard along the road, a phone call from someone who'd been relevant to my walk that day, or some other sort of synchronistic occurrence. It was as if these messages I was receiving in a quiet, sacred space were being reiterated as I reentered the real world, like signposts to guide my way. The synchronicity was constant and impossible to ignore, which allowed me to hear and hold on to these messages even amid the noise and distraction of daily life—of being constantly in mom mode, organizing everything, controlling everything (or attempting to, at least), and making sure that all facets of my sons' lives ran as smoothly as possible so that everything wouldn't fall apart around us.

At first I thought this experience was unique to me. Then, as time went on, as the labyrinth showed me how to quiet and heal myself in a holistic way, and as my coaching career took off, I realized that what I had actually been given was a method to get quiet so that I could really hear. Over time, I began sharing this same method with my clients, sometimes physically walking with them through the labyrinth, as well as leading retreats there, and at other times applying the quieting sequence of the paths in some of the ways we'll discuss later in this chapter. Witnessing the lives, hearts, and souls of these people settle in the same way mine did has been a profoundly powerful and joyful experience.

Today, both the labyrinth and the lessons it has taught me are ingrained in my heart and soul, kind of like an old friend I know so well that we pick up right where we left off every time we meet again, no matter how much time has passed between visits. Though what I now call the Get Quiet Way is labyrinth-inspired, my experience of walking its paths now comes with me through every step I take in the outside world. What I could once hear only in the labyrinth I can now hear as I walk about my daily life because the quietness it's shown me has made me open and available to hear what the universe is whispering. The labyrinth is where I first felt and flexed those muscles, strengthening them to the point where using them is now a continuous practice that happens almost without me even realizing it. Prior to walking the labyrinth, most of the decisions I made in my life didn't get me where I wanted to go because they were made from a place of fear, scarcity, and stagnation. The labyrinth showed me how to make decisions from a place of love, abundance, and growth, and my life is entirely changed because of it.

I return to the labyrinth whenever I need a clear answer or a shift in perspective, when I want to feel close to my spirit team and God, or whenever it calls for me to visit. And when that call comes, I can hear it loud and clear, thanks to the gifts the labyrinth has given me—gifts that are available to you too.

The Legacy of the Labyrinth

The labyrinth's purpose felt so clear and meaningful to me that I didn't actually research its history until several months after I first started walking it. Once I did, I found the overlay between the labyrinth's historical meaning and intention and my own experience to be uncanny.

Today, labyrinths are most commonly associated with the Christian tradition, but they actually existed—at least as an idea—long before Christians adopted them around 300 C.E., once they could safely worship without fear of persecution. In fact, the labyrinth's history seems to date back four thousand years and across cultures, as evidenced by prehistoric rock carvings that appear to portray labyrinths in both India and Europe. Labyrinths were part of both Greek and Roman society, with their geometric patterns often depicted in mosaics.

Over the centuries, labyrinths have symbolized different things for different cultures and times. Greeks, for example, created labyrinths that included a series of options and dead ends. Their labyrinths were associated with lore about King Minos of Crete and the Minotaur monster, and carried negative connotations of fear and evil. As time passed, labyrinths came to be associated with more spiritual and meditative purposes. Christians adopted labyrinths as a sacred symbol that represented one's journey toward God. These Christian labyrinths were often built into the floors of churches and cathedrals, and the labyrinth spread even farther to places like North Africa and Java, as well as to Native Americans in the Southwest.

Today labyrinths can be found both inside and outside of sacred spaces, not only in temples and cathedrals, but also in gardens, in public sites such as schools, libraries, and hospitals, and on private properties. In these different contexts, the meaning and intent of walking the labyrinth can be unique and personal to the individual walking. No matter what religion you subscribe to or what beliefs you hold, walking the labyrinth can be seen as a type of pilgrimage toward transformation or enlightenment. It can be considered to have healing effects. It can also be a tool for stillness and contemplation, as the person walking the labyrinth can quiet their thinking mind and relax into the paths the labyrinth has set forth for them, which lead them on a meandering journey toward the center and then back out into the world again.

Although labyrinths have taken on many shapes over the years, the labyrinth as we think of it today is not a maze, but a pathway that offers just a single path to the center. In this book, we'll focus on the classical seven-circuit labyrinth, which consists of a series of circular paths, including the labyrinth's center (see image on page 33). Intentionally walking the labyrinth shifts us from the more analytical left side of the brain to the more spiritual and emotional right side of the brain. We emerge more awakened, focused, and peaceful. We feel happier, more optimistic, and more connected.

Over the years, I have come to think of the labyrinth as a portal between this reality and a different realm and dimension. I see it as opening up a private conversation between the person journeying through the labyrinth and the divine. This idea of portals is not a new one. Legend holds that Apollo—who was the god of the sun, light, and prophecy in Greek and Roman mythology—for example, is known for having the superpower of entering into portals. In these portals, God spoke to Apollo who, in turn, delivered God's divine messages to the people. While Apollo may be a myth, the point here is that this idea of portals has been in the human consciousness for millennia, dating back to a time when the world was much quieter and humans were presumably more connected to the earth and all of the seen and unseen energies around them.

In my experience, the portal that is the labyrinth offers extraordinary healing powers, and part of those healing powers is a reminder of who we are and how God delivered us into this life. He brought us in with everything we need to flourish in this dimension, with a mind, body, and soul that are designed to work holistically and in tandem. I know you may not feel like it right now, but the labyrinth will remind you that you have all the love, power, understanding, connection, and everything else you need to grow and fulfill your purpose in this lifetime encoded within you, just waiting for you to tap into it.

Getting Quiet in the Labyrinth

The Get Quiet Way I'll share with you in this book came to me in the labyrinth, almost as if I was being given the keys to a door I'd been trying to push open for as long as I can remember. After all the struggle and worry, suddenly it was just a matter of turning the lock open. The details of each path came to me over the course of years as I was ready to access new levels of quiet and connection. The Get Quiet Way ultimately brought me back to my true self and allowed me to create an expansive and purposeful life that I'm excited about every single day.

The labyrinth showed me how it felt to be lifted out of the busy-ness and complexity of the daily material world. It was the first place where I could feel a true sense of stillness and grounding, which allowed me to tune in to and hear myself, my soul's true calling, and the guides that supported me. While there have been a lot of messages over the years, the loudest and most resonant of them all was the message that *I was going to be okay—more than okay*. And you are too. Once you experience that feeling of deep, divine support and guidance for yourself—even just once— you will know that it's *possible* and that this energy is available for you to tap into in moments when you need it. In a world where we often don't feel supported, this changes everything.

Getting to this point is a layered process, and, as you'll see, each part of the process is built upon the foundation of the path that comes before. Throughout these pages I will connect each of the paths of the labyrinth with a specific energy point in the body and the healing that's available within it. First you'll learn how to quiet, connect, and tune in to your body, then your heart, and then your mind. From there you will have a new understanding of how to bring new things into your life more easily by connecting to the support and guidance from God, your guides, your intuition, and the universe. As you walk around each path, drawing closer and closer to the center of the labyrinth, you'll find yourself getting closer and closer to the truth of who you are—which is a bright, beautiful soul, an integral part of the divine tapestry of the universe. Along the way, you'll shed the pain and heaviness you've been carrying around for so long, and you'll be able to live in a lighter, more joyful way that silences so much of the noise you're driven by and fighting against today. You get to choose what you take with you as you walk this path and what to leave behind, whether it's old ways of thinking and being, long-held trauma, or outdated identities.

I've personally found walking the labyrinth and its winding paths to be a valuable tool for instilling and embodying the Get Quiet Way. However, please know that this is not essential. If you're near a physical labyrinth, you can walk it as I did, focusing on each energy center along its designated path. (If you're not sure if you live near a labyrinth, you can visit www.labyrinthlocator .com to search your area.) If you aren't near one, you can trace the labyrinth with your fingers or draw your own, referring to the labyrinth image on page 33 to help you. Or just know that the cadence of the book follows the cadence of the labyrinth, so you're "walking" it just by reading. Even if you do have access to a labyrinth, I recommend that you take a moment to trace the image of the labyrinth now before continuing on in the book to ground you in the pages that follow. You can also come back to this image as necessary to trace it and absorb its energy in moments when you're looking for a mood boost, increased focus, clarity, or calm.

In the next few chapters of this book—Part II, "Healing"—we will discuss the longer, outer paths of the labyrinth, which focus on cleansing and clearing energy that is stuck in your body to bring in healing, peace, and a greater sense of flow. You'll find that the chapters that discuss these outer paths are longer and more pragmatic to match the external paths of the labyrinth we're focusing on and the denser energy we're shifting and working with. Then in Part III, "Discovering," we'll move through the shorter, inner paths of the labyrinth and look at how the universal energies, your intuition, and your soul can now use that clear space to connect you to yourself and your purpose. Likewise, these chapters will be briefer and more esoteric, focusing more on your internal state and the lighter energies now flowing through you. Each chapter will begin with a short guide to orient you to the path on the labyrinth we are currently focusing on (just a note that the paths aren't laid out in sequential order; for example, the labyrinth begins at path 3 rather than path 1) and will also include a visualization to guide you through a healing exercise for the energy point the path is associated with.

1
2
3
4
5
6
7

PART II

HEALING

BEFORE YOU EVEN TAKE

YOUR FIRST STEP INTO

THE LABYRINTH, YOU ARE

WELCOMED AT ITS ENTRANCE

BY DIVINE ENERGY. IT'S AS

IF ALL OF THESE SPIRITUAL

HELPERS TAKE YOUR HAND

LIKE LONG-LOST FRIENDS.

CHAPTER THREE

GET LIVING

Nurture Your Body

The life force within each of us is the greatest healer.

— HIPPOCRATES, ANCIENT GREEK PHYSICIAN

Walking the Labyrinth

Tune in to and vitalize your life force energy.

We begin our journey at the mouth of the labyrinth on path 3. Though this is the first path we'll walk, it's located toward the middle of the labyrinth. This is fitting because we're entering the labyrinth from the middle of our journey in this human form, and the labyrinth is meeting us where we are in this precise moment.

This path is associated with our physical vessel, the body. It's our body that allows us to have this human experience through which our soul learns, grows, and evolves. As we turn our attention to the body, we're focusing specifically on the abdomen. Just as this path of movement is situated in the center of the labyrinth, the abdomen is our body's center place, and it also houses the womb, where life—this physical manifestation of ourselves—begins.

It's here on this first circle around the labyrinth that we shake our bodies back to life again.

So much of getting quiet is a spiritual practice of realigning with yourself so that you can align with the loving forces that guide you and are longing to offer their support. As you approach the labyrinth for the first time, your energy is fragmented; you feel all over the place, as if you've lost both your identity and your way. Your body, mind, and soul all feel the impact of this, but right now all you're thinking about is how your body feels heavy, dense, and stuck. There is no sense of fluidity in, or even attachment to, this vessel you live in. You've given so much of yourself away that there never seems to be time to tend to yourself, even in the most basic of ways.

Before you even take your first step into the labyrinth, you are welcomed at its entrance by divine energy. It's as if all of these spiritual helpers take your hand like long-lost friends, and you can feel the playful, joyous energy seeping out of them and into you. You know with all of your heart that they only want what is good and meant for you.

You need to regather yourself, to find that center place in your body, in your being, so that you can once again create a sense of wholeness, of belonging to yourself. This is where the healing begins.

Beginning with the Body

It might surprise you to know that this spiritual work starts in a very physical way. That's why we're focusing on connecting with, moving, and nourishing the body to begin this journey, the dense matter that houses the light of your soul. Somewhat counterintuitively, you have to drop into this human experience to experience the divine.

What I'm really talking about here is the mind-body-soul connection. Most of us are aware of this concept on some level by now, but I do believe that we still don't quite understand it wholly or correctly. We tend to think about the mind, body, and soul as related yet still separate entities. In reality, there's no separation between the three at all. Your mind, body, and soul are intricately and inextricably meshed together. If one of these elements is not healthy and whole, the other two cannot be healthy or whole either. Everything we think and every emotion we feel is experienced in our body; everything we feel physically has an impact on our soul and our mind, and so on. No matter how strong your spiritual practice is, if you don't care for your body, your mind and soul will feel the impact.

When you begin to move and reconnect with your body, it will open you up to begin to heal emotionally and spiritually as well—whether that's your intention or not. If you can't feel your body, that means you also can't feel the energy in your body. When you start to move and reunite with your body, your energy shifts into a more natural alignment, which allows you to use this density you've been given to tap into the more subtle energy that exists both within and around you. In other words, when you move and become more aware of and connected to your body, you will begin to feel your emotions (which are, after all, just energy in motion) in addition to other signs, signals, and cues that are dulled when you're not truly connected and rooted in this beautiful body you've been given.

On some level, most of us intuitively understand this connection. Have you ever noticed that when you want to heal some sort of emotional pain, loss, or disappointment or otherwise move your life forward, you feel called to start moving your body? Through my work, I've come to understand that when a client tells me that they've just signed up for their first yoga class in years or have purchased new athletic shoes because they want to start walking regularly, it's a sign that they're ready to start doing the work of healing and getting quiet. But often they don't understand this themselves—they just know that they suddenly feel the urge to change something about their physical state.

If you think back on your own life, you might find that during times when you've wanted to heal pain or disappointment or make a big change, you've started with something physical. We instinctively start with the body because we humans tend to think of our bodies as the strongest, most "real" part of who we are. Both in my own life and in my work with healing, I've seen that this is not the case—our bodies are no stronger or more real than our souls. At the same time, we take these bodies of ours for granted. We ignore our body, beat it up, and feel resentful and deflated if it's somehow different from how we want it to be. Even for those of us who escape this human experience relatively unscathed by serious illness or injury, our body bears the brunt of a lot of pressure, wear, and tear in a lifetime—childbirth, more minor injuries, and the stress and pressure of daily life. Not to mention those emotions we don't acknowledge and heal, which often go on to manifest in a physical form. Our bodies are strong, but ultimately they're only temporary, and they need our loving attention along the way. Ultimately, they will age and weaken until the soul is once again set free. It's the soul that overrides everything, while the body is a critical yet temporary vessel. We need to celebrate, be compassionate with, and revel in this body while we have it.

Wherever you are right now, wherever you're trying to go, whatever needs to shift, the first thing you need to do is to *feel alive again*. You need to feel connected and whole, full and at peace in this beautiful body of yours that has been—and will continue to be—with you for every single second of this story you're writing called life.

Whatever brings you to this point of seeking quiet, chances are you're longing for something, yet perhaps unsure precisely what that something is or what the journey will entail. You just know *something* is missing. Now is the time for you to clean and clear, to feel lighter within your body so that it can nourish and unite with that beautiful soul of yours at its center. So many of our bodies are missing their soulmate in the most literal way possible, because if we're not truly inhabiting our body, we can't connect with our soul.

While you may or may not be literally walking a labyrinth as part of your Get Quiet experience, it's no accident that the labyrinth is a movement practice. Whether you walk the labyrinth or not as you navigate these pages, movement is still the first essential step. That might mean walking, stretching, swimming, or any other form of movement and flow that feels gentle and nurturing to you (more on that soon). This book is about shifting energy, and movement is the most foundational and essential way to do this. Moving your body allows you to feel good—something we too easily take for granted. It might sound simplistic, but feeling good is important; it's why you have a body in the first place!

Finally, movement is also a way of reminding yourself that if something doesn't move, it can't change.

Walking the Path of the Abdomen

The path of movement is associated with the energy point located in your abdomen. For our purposes, this area extends from just below the lungs down to directly above your tailbone. Your main source of power and energy dwells here in the center of your body. The abdomen represents your powerful life force because it holds the womb, where life originates. Maybe you're starting off from a place where it feels like your body is the enemy. Or maybe something just feels physically "off," and you're fatigued as a result or can't seem to find the energy and enthusiasm for life that you once had. You might feel disconnected from yourself or from the world you physically live in.

When your body needs attention, it will speak to you. Through both my work and my own experience as a human with a body, I have learned that many body-related issues present themselves through the abdomen. Over the years I've worked with women who can't get pregnant for any number of reasons; there is often an emotional reason as well, such as long-held trauma that is keeping the womb area devoid of free-flowing energy. Or they might have a weak liver from taking in too many toxins to the point where their body is overloaded and can no longer detoxify itself like it's designed to do. They might be experiencing digestive or autoimmune diseases. The list goes on.

Sometimes these ailments are less physical yet still tied to the abdominal area. Perhaps you feel stagnant in life. You might feel unhappy or uncomfortable in your body. Maybe you're suffering from a lack of power in your home, job, or life. You could be feeling lethargic, like you don't have the energy to move, let alone engage with life in the way you want to. If any of this rings true to you, know that all of these issues ultimately have to do with the energy center that lies in your abdomen, and you heal the abdomen by embodying movement and fluidity.

The abdomen is the largest area of your physical form, and it holds many of your essential organs, including your liver, stomach, and intestines. A lot of movement, supportive functions, and *life* happen in this area. Your abdomen houses everything essential to life outside of your brain and heart. It's where your power begins, and it's also a place where you can lose power through stagnation. This area of your body is not designed to be stagnant; it's designed for movement—literally in terms of how it moves nutrients through your body and supports your physical structure and also figuratively in terms of moving you forward in life. Life is created in this area, and it's also where creativity in general is contained. It's the area of the body where your dreams rest. Clarity and information are available to you when you tap into your gut, the second brain that dwells in your microbiome and is far more instinctual and attuned to everything around you than the "thinking" brain that lives in your head. It's also deeply connected to your emotional state. There's that mind-body-soul connection in action!

We don't talk enough about how easy it is to lose touch with all the power our body has to offer—and that's especially true when it comes to women who have given birth. Motherhood is an amazing, beautiful gift, *and* it can also deplete us on every level, in ways we're not even aware of until years down the line. When we're so busy with the physical work of caring for and nurturing others, often to our own detriment, it can be easy to give all of our power and energy away, both literally and figuratively, and to lose our connection with ourselves in the process.

For as essential as the abdomen is to vitality, creativity, and power, it's also the area of the body that many women are most critical of. We focus so much judgment on how our belly looks and changes over time. The truth of the matter is that women tend to gain weight around their midsection. We bloat during certain parts of our cycle, keep weight on after pregnancy, and gain weight during menopause. All of this is how we're built as women. It's part of our life cycle and creative process. Through each and every one of these phases and transformations, it's important to love yourself and see your own beauty in all its changing forms so that you can share it with the world.

Visualization for the Abdomen

Settle in to a calm and steady breath and bring your attention to your abdomen. When you feel ready, begin sending loving energy to this area of your body. This energy is so real and healing that you can feel it as if a warm, soothing ray of light is radiating healing energy throughout your belly. Continue sending love to your midsection and feeling the warm light spread.

Now imagine a beautiful flower growing right there, in the middle of your abdomen. Notice that you are able to take hold of the flower's stem and gently but firmly pull it up and out through your belly button. Look around and notice if there are any other flowers that need to be picked. Continue to pull them up and out one by one until the region feels clean and clear. Once you have finished, return to your breath and that healing ray of light. Notice all of the space you've created and any way in which the energy of your midsection now feels different than it did when you started.

Coming Home

Rather than seeing our body as the beautiful vehicle it is, we women tend to spend our time picking it apart. "I'm too *this*" or "I'm not enough of *that*." We analyze and disparage ourselves from head to toe, often putting a particularly unforgiving focus on the abdomen. But what if we instead shifted our perception to what really matters about our body? What if we looked at it and noticed the life force it gives us and reflected on how it's been with us—growing, changing, and evolving—for our entire lives? What if we focused on the fact that our body can generate, and perhaps *has* generated, new life, new bodies that can also walk upon this planet and that house other bright souls who have come here to live, love, and learn? What if we considered how much gratitude we should have for these bodies that animate our souls?

Our bodies are the most visible, obvious things about us, and yet so many women hide their bodies for any number of reasons. When we do this, we separate ourselves from our body. This separation from the body can happen in subtle ways, like when a woman holds a purse in front of her stomach or strategically positions herself behind someone else in pictures. There have been plenty of times when I haven't felt great about myself because I ate "too much" at a meal or the scale was 20 pounds heavier than I wanted it to be. In moments like this, I have considered hiding out, backing out of an engagement where I could potentially help people because I didn't want to be seen. Can you relate?

This behavior might seem innocuous enough, but you know the saying: as within, so without. When you hide your body, you hide yourself. You hide your greatness from the world. Your body is the container through which you get to enact your gifts and your purpose in the world. You were born into this body to have this life experience, and it is meant to be fully inhabited so that you can enjoy all the experiences this life has to offer, and if you're hiding in any way, how can you ever fulfill all of your beautiful potential? It's a way of staying small, of shrinking, rather than standing proudly in your embodied state. You can't hide and be in your power and greatness at the same time. Don't miss out on all of the beauty and learning that's meant for you in 3D form.

WHAT'S EATING YOU?

The next time you find yourself feeling like you want to hide or shrink, rather than thinking about what you're eating, instead think about what's eating you.

Find a spot where you can get comfortable and sit with your thoughts. Close your eyes and take a deep breath in. Feel yourself sink into your body as you place your hands gently on your belly. Notice what you're feeling and get curious about that. What might be causing you to feel this way? Take an even deeper breath in, and as you exhale, allow that out-breath to clear your mind. Now ask yourself: *What's eating me?*

Listen to the answer, and take a few moments to sit with what you hear. When you feel ready, focus on sending love and compassion to yourself through your healing hands. Feel the loving energy as it moves through your belly and, from there, outward to your entire body. As you feel the loving energy course through you, repeat to yourself: *Only the love I have for myself can truly heal me.*

The saying goes that your body is a temple, but I think it's much more than that. Though it *is* sacred, your body is your *home.*

How does your body, your home, feel to you? Dusty and full of cobwebs? Cramped and haphazard? Like you're just renting out the space?

How do you want your home to feel? Really stop and consider that for a moment. Do you feel strong? Are you able to move through your day with ease, accomplishing all that you want to do? Do you feel beautiful and connected with your femininity? If the answer to any of these questions is no, it's a message that your body needs some care and attention. Among other things, I would imagine that, as with any home, you want to feel safe in your body. Home should be a place where you can feel completely at ease and relaxed, knowing that you are in a safe haven. It should be comfortable, peaceful, open, and inviting.

Now think about how much attention you pay to your actual material home. How much effort do you put into maintaining it and making it feel fresh and clean, like a healthy sanctuary? Most of us take care of our home for ourselves, yes, but also because we know that other people we care about live in, use, and visit it. But are you taking care of your own home—your body—with the same degree of attention and care?

However you want your body to feel, keep that at the top of your mind as you walk through your day and make your choices accordingly. Start to build the habit of being aware of your body, how it feels, and what it needs. Just like you would notice when clutter needs to be picked up and put away or items need to be shifted or cleaned in your house, notice when it feels like something in your body needs attention—and then offer it. What can you do to feel safe? To feel comfortable and peaceful? To feel whatever it is you want to feel in this home of yours that's constructed of flesh and blood? And how can you move or nurture your body to lead yourself further in that direction?

Remember, You're Alive!

Of course you're aware of the fact that you're alive. But do you really *feel* a sense of vitality and animation on a moment-to-moment basis? Do you stop to appreciate what a gift it is to have this body that's guided you through so much already and that will continue to guide you through so much more in the future? Your body is *such* a gift, and yet it's so easy to take this essential *aliveness* for granted.

Many women start to think of their body as a tool, often without even being consciously aware of that fact. A tool that will get them all of the places they need to go and allow them to perform all of the functions that need to be done on a day-to-day basis—functions at home, at work, and in the world. And when we *do* focus on our body, it's often not in a gentle and loving way. Instead we try to "fix" our bodies, to wield them into a certain shape that we feel we must attain. That's not the kind of movement or attention I'm talking about here.

Your body stores so much physical, mental, and emotional residue. You are quite literally holding stress and excess adrenaline in your body, and if you're not moving it out, that means it's stuck and locked in. This is true on both a physical and energetic level. Think about the language we use when something difficult befalls us in life: gut punch, broken heart, head spinning. All of this involves a feeling of stuckness, of disorientation, and the inability to move forward. The only way to disperse that energy is to move it around, to literally shake it off. Think back to a time when you've felt so extremely nervous or anxious that your body has started to tremble or shake. This is your body's natural response at work, dispersing adrenaline and fear by relaxing muscle tension and calming the nervous system through a somatic response. In less extreme situations, your body won't initiate this shaking in an instinctual way, so it's up to you to proactively shake the energy off. Go ahead, I'll wait right here while you take a moment to shake—shake your arms, legs, hips, head, feet, and hands. Let's start releasing all of that pent-up stress and fear to free your body and your energy by allowing this somatic response. By doing this, you are giving your body the opportunity to release the energy it's been holding on to.

Once you have released this energy, you can then allow animation and flow to replace it through movement. As you incorporate movement into your life, remember that it's not for the purpose of "fixing" or "tweaking" anything about yourself. We've been so conditioned to use our time "productively," and to fit into a certain physical mold, that I find many of my clients initially come at movement with intensity. I did the same thing when I first integrated movement into my life as my marriage began to crumble. I get it: we want to feel power, shift things, burn off energy, and move forward. But if we come at movement with intensity, aggression, or purpose beyond the sheer pleasure of movement itself, it will only lead to more burnout, more pressure and expectation, and more stress on and in your body. It can add a sense of tightness and even more density, and it can become yet another item to check off your list. This sort of physical movement is like driving your car so fast that you don't even have the time or presence to notice, much less experience, the beautiful scenery around you. If you drive more slowly, on the other hand, you can actually take in the view around you.

Instead of speeding, pushing, or feeling stuck, imagine your body as a river of life. Rivers can be soft, flowing, and gentle, and yet they also move things through, both on and below the surface. They epitomize energy in motion. In your own body, this fluidity will move energy around to alleviate—and eventually dissipate—that sense of stuckness. Move slowly, gracefully, and consistently. Keep moving at your own pace and cadence, even during difficult moments. Movement is always important, but it's particularly important during difficult times to feel where things are stuck, unstick them, maintain your connection with yourself, and continue hearing what your body has to tell you—because it whispers to you for a reason and its messages are always important. If you are able to slow your physical body and keep it in flow, the deeper parts of you—your mind, emotions, and spirit—will follow.

Move your body in such a way that it feels like an act of kindness to yourself—gentle, supportive, and nurturing. It doesn't matter what that movement looks like, and it absolutely doesn't have to be regimented. It might not even involve *movement* as you currently think of it at all. I began feeling pleasure in my body by regularly incorporating baths into my routine—something I had rarely done for myself up to that point. A few nights a week, I closed my bedroom door and set up a beautiful bath for one, candles and all. In the twilight I caught glimpses of my wet body shimmering in the shadowy twinkle of the candlelight. In that soapy water, I allowed myself to see parts of my body that I had looked away from before. Like a child, I allowed myself to play in the water, feeling my body's lightness as I moved. I placed my hands on my abdomen and intentionally sent gratitude for the lives it had housed. The more I came to appreciate my body, the more I wanted to take care of it and to use it in the way it was designed—for nourishment, pleasure, and movement.

A walk or swim, some stretching. Pilates, yoga, and qigong are all supportive of your body. They bring you back to a sense of awareness of how it feels to be in your own skin and how your body moves; they call your attention to the ways in which your body and breath can mingle in perfect harmony. This kind of movement allows you to get quiet so that you can hear what your body is saying to you and understand what it needs. The more of your body that's involved in this movement, the better. As you move, think of the stress, adrenaline, and stagnant energy moving and dissipating. Take a deep breath in, and feel your heart rate begin to slow as your nervous system settles. When your nervous system relaxes, you can begin to establish that sense of safety within yourself.

Once you start moving in a way that is kind and gentle to your body and that acknowledges its presence and magnificence, it's almost impossible not to notice your vibrance and vitality. Movement will shake you awake to the understanding that the world has been living in a sort of zombie apocalypse and that you are not disempowered in the ways you might currently feel that you are. Movement is transformational—much more so than we tend to give it credit for.

My client Cynthia is a great example of how movement is often the solution we don't know we're looking for to shake ourselves back to life. As a married mother of a teenage son, Cynthia came to me because she felt powerless in her work and unappreciated at home. She wasn't embracing her power in any facet of her life, and she felt small. She didn't have a real understanding of what her gifts were; she didn't realize that she had the capacity to do great things in many areas of her life. From the outside, it didn't seem that Cynthia was powerless at all—she was a vice president of a Fortune 500 company, sat on a mission-driven board of directors, and regularly participated in missionary trips that fulfilled her passion to aid children living in poverty. But that didn't change how she *felt*. At work, all Cynthia could focus on was the fact that she wasn't president. At home, Cynthia felt guilty because her husband was resentful of her professional success and how many household duties he took care of when she was busy at work or traveling for her missionary efforts. On top of all of this, Cynthia didn't feel great physically. She focused all her time on everything and everyone else around her and ignored her body completely. She had kept extra weight on after childbirth, which made her feel uncomfortable in her own body, and she worried that her husband wasn't attracted to her like he'd once been.

Cynthia was convinced that the only solution to become unstuck was to leave her current role as the vice president of a prestigious company in order to find a "better job." She was sure that this move would somehow make her feel happier and more satisfied. But as Cynthia and I walked the labyrinth together, a clear message came through for her: *A change will do you good, but don't force it. I see you smiling and happy.* Even though it wasn't the message Cynthia had anticipated or hoped for, it seemed clear that changing jobs wasn't going to provide the shift that she was looking for in her life. From our conversations, I knew that she was always attending to someone or something else and completely dismissed taking care of herself in the process. How could she possibly feel a sense of power when there was nothing left for her? I suggested that Cynthia start much smaller and instead try moving a little bit each day to see if that made her feel any happier or more empowered.

When I suggested that bringing movement into her life would help her feel better, Cynthia's eyes widened. She already didn't have enough hours in the day! I assured her that it was all about consistency and that even small movements and a little bit of time would help. She started by taking six minutes to do some gentle stretching in the morning. Once she saw how the stretching made her feel, she agreed to carve out room in her schedule to get to the swimming pool regularly. She didn't start by swimming laps or doing anything intense; she simply focused on making time to move her body in the water on a regular basis. Before long,

Cynthia began to notice some beautiful changes: she felt reconnected with her femininity and had a new appreciation for how beautifully her body moved; she noticed how graceful she felt in the weightless water and the sense of lightness it infused in her. At first she only experienced these sensations in the pool, but after a few weeks, she started to notice them outside of the pool as well. She began to view her body as a beautiful instrument rather than resenting how it had changed over the years or ignoring it altogether. Cynthia realized how much power she had to tap into simply because she had this beautiful physical body.

Best of all, after a few weeks of regularly visiting the pool, Cynthia spoke of feeling a love and appreciation for herself that she'd never experienced before. She stopped beating herself up and judging herself as she had done before. This alone made her feel happier and healthier. The tension in her relationship melted away, and Cynthia and her husband began to experience a sense of closeness and intimacy they hadn't in years. She even found herself parenting differently due to this sense of flow and freedom she'd unearthed. "I feel alive again!" Cynthia exclaimed to me one day.

In the end, Cynthia stayed at her job . . . and was perfectly happy there because she now showed up in a new way thanks to this shift she'd had in perception. She was able to have a different, more empowered experience in her work because she'd figured out how to access a sense of confidence and trust in herself. She found that the stories she'd been telling herself about her job faded away as she got back into her body and became more present in the moment. Now, instead of feeling the need to jump around and make changes in her life during the moments when she felt unhappy or disempowered, Cynthia instead jumped into the pool and reconnected with herself.

Cynthia is not unique. I've seen many clients who believe that logistical elements of their life need to be shifted or changed in significant ways—be it a relationship or a job or their location—when, really, what they need is to reconnect with and start taking care of themselves. By starting at that point, they set a cascade effect in motion, and other things begin to change and shift and flow as well. Sometimes my clients do ultimately decide to make changes in their lives, yes, but those changes are often not what they would have initially believed them to be, and any changes they decide to make come from a more centered, empowered, and purpose-filled place. Because, as we all know, you take yourself wherever you go.

Listening to Heal Your Body

Once you step back into your body through movement, you'll be able to hear what your body is saying in a new way. For many people, this means noticing ways in which they're undernourished or simply becoming consciously aware of things that have been "off" for so long that they've accepted not feeling their best as status quo. For others, this means cultivating the awareness to understand when symptoms in their body are pointing to bigger issues.

Even subtle sensations are important guideposts to point you toward healing. Healing may mean a lot of things, and while aches and pains can sometimes be the result of purely physical issues, they often guide us toward emotions that need to be acknowledged, processed, and healed so that emotions aren't ignored to the point where they become physical manifestations. (More on this in the next chapter.) The more attuned to your physical body you become, the more you will be able to hear and respond to its whispers, like the dull ache of a broken heart, as opposed to getting to the point where the body is resigned to screaming its message, like a heart attack.

Too often I see people looking away from the issues their body is desperately trying to alert them to and instead focusing on superficial physical features that don't really matter. I get it; it can feel easier to focus on your graying hair than the mass on your neck. But plain and simple, this is fear—fear of what our bodies have to say to us and a sense of overwhelm that something is wrong. The more you move and connect with your body, the less apt you are to ignore its messages, and the more likely you are to be in relationship with it. There's nothing to fear, though; your body wants you to listen to it so that it can point you in the direction of healing. That's why it's speaking to you and calling for your attention.

In addition to being able to more easily understand when your body is calling out for attention and care, you may also very well find that you start to become aware of things that are impacting your body that you looked away from before. This might involve your diet, medication, supplements, recreational substances, media, environmental elements, and habits, among many other things. Anything that you consume, whether literally or figuratively, has an effect on your body. As you become more connected to your body and hear what it has to say, you can shift your choices from there. Many of my clients are shocked once they reach this point of greater attunement and become consciously aware of habits they've fallen into that don't actually make their body feel good. Yet, to this point, they've continued to do them anyway, often without thinking twice. Over time they've started to assume that the lethargy, depression, anxiety, or chronic pain they feel is simply the way it will always be. More often than not, it turns out this isn't the case at all.

When I was diagnosed with Hashimoto's disease, I was put on one of the most popular medications in the U.S. to manage my thyroid function. For more than a decade, I went into the local pharmacy once every month to refill my medication. When I walked the labyrinth one morning, I very clearly heard the message *Don't take your medicine*. This guidance went against everything I had been taught up to that point, which is that if you're on medication, you take it every single day. I sat with the message for a few minutes and then suddenly understood that all I was doing with this medication was swallowing my health problems, one handful at a time, every single day. I decided to do something I'd never done before and skipped my medicine. I felt *great*! I didn't feel sluggish like I had grown so accustomed to feeling, nor did I feel the physical depression that had lingered over me for so long. I felt awake, happy, and energetic, even! All of this was subtle but also significant. It was as if the sense of heaviness I'd been carrying around for years had suddenly lifted. Once it did, I found myself in disbelief that I'd been living like that for all these years when I now literally felt better overnight after a single missed pill.

I was simultaneously delighted and confused about why this might be the case. How could my body feel better without the medicine I'd been told to take? I decided to research. As I began to educate myself, I realized how blindly I'd been taking medicine without really understanding what I was putting into my body. I had only paid attention to the promise of the active ingredient without ever even considering the inactive ingredients or excipients (these are the filler ingredients that do things like help the medication bind, be more easily consumed, and taste better). It turned out that there were several inactive ingredients in this single medication I was taking. As I realized this, everything seemed so much clearer—my body is sensitive, and I knew myself well enough to understand that it wouldn't react well to all of these ingredients flooding my body on a daily basis.

My sense was that I *would* benefit from the active ingredient, but not the others, so I talked with my doctor, who suggested I take a compounded version of the medication—a version that contains the active ingredient that supported my thyroid, along with a few necessary natural inactive ingredients, and without all of the rest of the junk that had been sitting in my body for years now.

I continued to feel better and better as time went by: more energetic, lighter, brighter, more vibrant, and more curious about life. There was almost an innocence to it. *I remember you*, the voice in my head said. After all this time, I had forgotten how it felt to be *me*—alert, alive, and aglow—and feeling that version of myself reemerge was profound. I now understand that she was there all along, just waiting to feel safe and at home in my body once again so that the second verse of my life could begin. She is my nature, the purest version of me, without all of the heaviness.

I'm far from alone in this experience of creating a massive positive shift in the state of my body from a relatively minor tweak once bodily awareness sets in. Experiencing this rush of wellness feels fantastic to the point where it's almost like a rebirth. And yes, it can also be scary. Once all of the filler medications were out of my body and I felt reenergized, it dawned on me that I could now play a bigger game with all of this newly rediscovered energy and vitality. My body felt ready to do more and to do it better . . . and with this came an unexpected tinge of fear. Although it had been unconscious at the time, I could now see that I'd spent years relying on this sense of sickness as a crutch. For all that time, I couldn't do or stick with many things because I didn't feel well or because I was tired or didn't have the energy. *When we're sick we're safe from fear because the sickness occupies us.* We don't have to risk fear or failure because our attention is solely focused on what ails us. This wasn't an entirely new realization for me; I'd seen it with my clients but hadn't yet recognized it in myself. I had unconsciously done what I'd seen others do, which is to wrap my entire identity around a chronic disease. Now that this black cloud of thyroid medication had lifted, I could see the potential this new surge of energy and wellness allowed me. It was exciting and also scary because now I had no more excuses. I was free to build a new identity that wasn't limited by the sickness that I'd allowed to hold me back.

Of course, no one consciously wants to live in a body that feels sick, but so many people have a similar experience to mine. It's as if our body hangs on to illness and even creates an identity around it so that it can feel "safe" from having the capacity to live out its greatest potential—and perhaps failing in the process. And yet we must. We are in this body, in this life, for the express reason that we have a unique purpose to fulfill. The healthier our bodies are, the more accessible that purpose is.

Many women are carrying around their own heaviness. They've been carrying it for so long that they barely even recognize it's there most of the time. Instead, they feel like I did: like they can't muster up the energy to do anything more than the have-tos (and boy, are there plenty of those!), like they're always feeling a bit fuzzy or uncomfortable in their own body. Not all of these ailments are debilitating—but they *do* have a cumulative impact. So they learn to power through the heaviness or the discomfort or even the pain, so it often doesn't occur to them that there could be a reason for it, and, at the end of the day, it could even be a reason that's pretty simple and resolvable. But, like me, when they do get to the root of the issue—when they figure out the food, medication, habit, or environment that's in misalignment with their body—that subtle shift can be profound.

No matter how you feel today, know that it's possible to go from feeling bad to feeling good—no matter how daunting or even impossible that seems from where you stand. Getting to this healthier, more vibrant state may very well not take as much as you might think. So much of nurturing your physical body involves a mindset shift and the willingness to prioritize yourself on a consistent basis. Once you start doing this, I bet you'll find that you have more energy, a new sense of freedom in and appreciation for this beautiful body of yours, and renewed confidence and strength. It's hard to believe how many areas of your life a healthier, freer body will positively impact. And most important, it will improve your appreciation of yourself.

LOOK FOR THE BEAUTY

THAT'S ALL AROUND YOU

IN EVERY MOMENT OF

EVERY DAY IF ONLY YOU'RE

OPEN TO RECEIVING IT.

THE MORE YOU SEE AND

FEEL THIS BEAUTY, THE

MORE YOU WILL EMBODY IT.

CHAPTER FOUR

GET ENERGIZED

Your Environment Paves the Way to an Open Heart

The goal is to make your heartbeat match the beat of the universe, to match your nature with nature.

— JOSEPH CAMPBELL, AUTHOR

Walking the Labyrinth

Quiet your heart and breath as you walk this path to sync your breath with the divine.

Your heart and lungs—the parts of you that energize and animate your body, that serve as your essential life forces—are associated with path 2 of the labyrinth. As you make your way from path 3 to path 2, from the abdomen to the heart, you find yourself in a larger, more exterior circle. Here, you are removed from the outside world by only one singular remaining path. Out here, close to the life outside the labyrinth, you might feel vulnerable, and yet there is an opportunity to heal and connect to the greater world around you even as you connect more intimately to the loving energy of God and the universe, matching the rhythm of your heart and breath with that of the divine.

Soon after my divorce, I found myself sitting alone in a movie theater, crying as I watched the movie *It's Complicated*, a romantic comedy about a divorced couple. By the time I noticed I was crying, my face was already wet to the touch. Feeling these tears shocked me. Despite (or, more accurately, *because* of) the pain I'd experienced leading up to, during, and in the wake of my divorce, I hadn't cried once throughout the entire process or at any point during the year that followed.

Until now.

Here I was bawling to the point where I could barely make out the images on the screen in front of me. It felt wonderful, and even energizing, as if something had finally cracked through the walls I had carefully constructed around my heart without even fully realizing it. I craved love, and at the same time I couldn't imagine experiencing the pain I now associated with love ever again, and so I'd built those walls in an effort to keep pain at bay. But really, all I had been doing was locking that pain and hurt in close to my heart. It couldn't get out, and also, nothing else could get in. All of that heavy, dark, and fearful energy just sat there filling up my chest, with no release, nowhere else to go.

Through those tears there was release. Of course, they were a drop in the ocean, but still, they were a start. As I walked out of the theater and into the heat of the Arizona night, I felt lighter, a bit more buoyant. Yes, my face was still tear-streaked, but I also felt a smile sweeping across my face. That also felt foreign. It wasn't that I hadn't smiled at all over these past few years, but it hadn't been a smile like this—a smile that just placed itself on my face for no apparent reason.

I felt a sense of freedom for the first time in a long time, because I was *feeling* for the first time in a long time. Something in me had given way. And that made me feel like *myself* again, which was the best part of it all. It felt like . . . possibility.

It's interesting that during the most intense periods of our lives, the times when we expect to feel the most emotions, so often we're actually feeling the least. Notice the word *feeling* here: it's not that the emotions aren't present, but that we're not allowing ourselves to feel them. If we're not feeling our emotions, that means we also can't process them and heal them. It's almost as if we become overwhelmed by the feeling of it all, by our fear of pain, and we go into a system overload in response.

I've certainly experienced this, and I've also found it's a common experience for my clients and women in general. Our chest area, where the heart and lungs live, is blocked and closed off because we have loved and are now finding our way through grief and loss. As a result, we numb out and keep running to avoid the pain. Our hearts (in other words, our internal environments) become cluttered with all of this unhealed emotion, which tends to manifest in an external environment that feels cluttered as well. This external clutter can consist of any number of things in the environment where you dwell or work: home repairs that go ignored, the tsunami of e-mails in your inbox, the way in which you're consuming media, the expired food in your pantry, or the humans that share your space.

Both your internal and external environments are either healthy or they're vulnerable, and one generally reflects the other. When you don't clear your space and tend to the clutter, it's easy to fall into a pattern of feeling stuck and uneasy as a result. If it's not tended to, this kind of environment threatens to control you, keeping you in a chaotic cycle.

The good news is that *you* get to choose your environment, even if it doesn't feel like it in this precise moment. You have control of your heart and of your home. Once you choose to claim control of your environment, you can relax into your brilliance, clearing the channels within you to flow freely so that your entire life moves to the beat of the unique rhythm of your heart.

Walking the Path of the Heart

Our heartbeat and breath both emanate from our chest, the part of the body this path is associated with. These are the essential functions that keep our bodies alive, animated, and functioning in this earthly form. It makes sense that we're protective of this area of our body, both physically and energetically. After all, our very survival depends on it.

And yet, all of that protection ultimately leads to residue and corrosion. It's like the emotional and energetic version of building up plaque around the heart or in the lungs. When you allow this to happen without noticing or intervening, your heartbeat and breath can't support you with their beautiful natural rhythm. Just like you experience physical pain and discomfort when an area of your body needs attention, you also experience pain and cues about what needs to be addressed through your emotions—which are energy, just like physical pains are. From a purely energetic standpoint, the chest is an area of our bodies where we all—and especially us women—hold so much stuck energy. When you don't allow yourself to feel these symptoms so that you can alleviate the blockage, your emotional and energetic health suffer.

Now that you are feeling attuned to your body, you may find that you are also suddenly more attuned to your heart and breath, because that kinetic energy you've created through movement naturally begins to seep into other areas of your life. However, it may very well not be clear that this is what's happening; instead, you might simply notice that you have an urge to move not just your body, but other things around you as well. In other words, you have the urge to start shifting your environment. If this sounds very literal, that's because these outer layers of the labyrinth often are. For me, once I found a sense of home in my body, I was more attuned to my reactions to the various elements of life and, most specifically, my environment—in this case, my home.

In the daily rush of day-to-day life, it can be easy to overlook the very real impact of our physical environment, but it's no joke. I want to be very clear that creating a sense of beauty and order in your physical space that allows you to relax and surrender is not a luxury or something that should be constantly pushed down your to-do list in favor of "more pressing" items. It is *deeply* important to create a space that feels beautiful, clean, calm, and inviting to you. I'm not suggesting that you do this by spending a lot of money to refurbish your home. In fact, once you tune in to your environment, you may very well find that what you're craving is expunging rather than bringing in, having less and not more. What you need to clear and refresh in your physical environment will be specific to you, and even if you don't know exactly what that is right now, it will reveal itself as you start taking tiny steps toward adjusting your space. You can take the time to stop and notice how each of those changes *feels*. Do you feel lighter? Like you can breathe a bit more freely? A sense of calm? More in control? Notice and acknowledge each little shift you feel with each change you make, no matter how small.

I first discovered the importance and impact of beautifying my surroundings when I went from living in a large, extravagant home to a small two-bedroom for me and my two young sons. Once I wielded control over that environment (and, by extension, my internal environment), I was far happier in that simple, cozy little place than I ever was in my previous more luxurious surroundings. I discovered that I responded much better to an environment that was clean and intentional, with little touches that meant something to me—like fresh herbs growing in the windowsill that added a splash of greenery, smelled delicious every time I walked by, and added a homegrown burst of flavor to our meals—than I ever did in a place that was all about more, more, more. What mattered is that I was present and intentionally creating a space that was nourishing to me and my family, rather than existing in a state of chaos and overwhelm that didn't feel like a true reflection of me or my family.

Creating this kind of environment doesn't mean that you can (or should remotely attempt to) control *everything* outside of yourself. Instead, your physical space will offer you a reprieve, a place where you can relax and surrender. It will feel like a haven where you can safely heal and transmute any painful energy that might exist in your body.

As I became more attuned to my body, I found myself suddenly becoming more aware of the environment around me, noticing all of the things that had gone by the wayside in those years when I'd felt so stuck. I couldn't stop cleaning and clearing my home and moving furniture around (and sometimes out of) the house altogether—for reasons I couldn't understand, it felt almost vital. For me, this usually meant taking out the old to bring in the new—cleaning out clothes in the closet that I no longer wore, clearing the kitchen cupboards of food that had lingered for too long, and removing trinkets from my home that reminded me of the past. In clearing out these physical things, I was moving out old, stale, stuck energy, which ultimately gave me the opportunity to decide whether or not I wanted to bring in something new.

When I was just trying to make ends meet and not really present in my own life, none of this seemed to matter so much—and it certainly wasn't anywhere near a top priority. Which makes sense, because our environment is a reflection of what and how we're feeling. When you are stuck, so is your environment. This often means holding on to things, and those things stagnate the space around you. They embody the energy of resisting change. You might be surprised how quickly and drastically that can change, though. Once I started clearing my space, I became so attuned to the energy around me that my kids would often joke, "Oh, God. There goes Mom moving the furniture around again." To this day, they ask what we're moving when they come to visit me.

All of this is about so much more than just chucking old clothes into a bag to haul them to a donation center. It's about sorting through, outfit by outfit, shoe by shoe, forgotten box by forgotten box, and remembering who you were in those moments of life, what you've survived, the joys you've experienced, and the wisdom you hold. It's an opportunity to unearth parts of yourself that you may have lost along the way. For example, one day I opened up a dusty box from my childhood that was filled with pictures and letters from my past from people who are no longer here, like my grandparents. Looking through these old relics offered me a glimpse of who I was in my natural state, someone I'd all but forgotten.

CORNERS TO CLEAR

Until you begin to clear your space, it's possible to miss the fact that you're basically living in a home straight out of *Hoarders*! While I'm kidding, it's easy to underestimate all of the different corners of our life that will benefit from some cleaning and clearing. Here are some places to start, some that are physical spaces and others that are digital but still make up an impactful part of your environment.

Home

- Closets

- Drawers

- Pantry

- Refrigerator (don't just clear the food, but also clean each shelf)

- Outside storage units

- Car (inside and out)

Digital space

- Electronic devices, including your phone and computer (delete outdated contacts, documents, pictures, and so on)

- Media exposure

- Social media (accounts and followers)

By nature, we are attuning our senses when we take control of our environment. To understand what is and is not aligned with us—what needs to go and what needs to stay—means that we must be acutely aware of the sights, sounds, smells, tastes, movements, and sensations around us. As you notice these things, you will also cultivate a greater sense of what's uniquely important to you when it comes to environmental wellness. For example, maybe you're not significantly impacted by the sounds around you, but it's very important that you be surrounded by scents that enhance your desired state (relaxed, energized, and so on). Or maybe you notice that an easy antidote to any sense of overwhelm or stress you might feel is holding your purring cat in your arms and being aware of how the rhythm of its purr feels against your skin, how its soft fur feels under your fingertips.

You can also start to tune in to how you want your space to feel so that it sparks the energy you're looking to ignite for you and your loved ones. My grandmother (whom I called Nana) was masterful at this. Some of my favorite childhood memories happened in her home, and I can still easily connect with that sense of love I felt every time I walked through her door. You could *feel* how healthy and flowing her home was. Looking back, I believe this is because she set up what I think of as different "zones" in each room of her house. She was very deliberate and intentional about what went where, and each room evoked a specific emotion and energy as a result. For example, her kitchen was always stocked with ingredients to cook and bake, and there was always a great smell wafting out of the room, inviting you into a cocoon of warmth and nourishment. Her art room was adorned with oil paintings and vibrant colors everywhere and always stocked with paints and blank canvases. Just being in there made your creativity spark to life. Her house was modest and simple, but that didn't matter, because every corner of it was curated with a tangible sense of intention and purpose. Think about all of the different ways you want to feel in your own home, and then create spaces that match that feeling. Then notice how things start to shift in your heart and in your life.

As I worked on my own environment, there was no mistaking the fact that the more I allowed it to be fluid, to notice how it was making me feel, and to make changes and create space as I saw fit, the better I felt. I didn't realize it at the time, but it's almost as if I was titrating myself to change by doing this. I was a "memory hoarder" who had to be forced into change kicking and screaming. Now instead of holding on to a time capsule, I was purging and creating space for new memories to come in. Sometimes I chose to refill that space I had created with something that felt truer to where and who I was in that moment; other times it felt good to leave that space there—open, airy, and inviting. I found that when I did all of these things, the house felt "healthier" somehow, just as my nana's had—not just for me, but for my boys, too.

And then something interesting happened. I noticed that the more intentional I was about my personal space, the more other parts of my life started to clear and open up. If my house felt healthier with a bit of rearranging, then perhaps my heart and soul could too. After all, it's all just energy, right? So, I started to feel into myself, to identify the places where I felt "cluttered," as if my energy was stuck. I focused on moving that energy through, on making shifts in my emotional state just as I had done in my physical state. Instead of blocking and avoiding feelings like I had been before by cramming them into the corners of my heart, I opened the door and examined them. I looked at each emotion and felt its texture, just like I had done with the clothes in my closet. I considered whether it was a relic from my past that I could release or an emotion that I wanted to bring forward with me. This process took some time and patience, and I had to walk away from it and then come back to it many times. But by the time I finished, I had a bright, fresh, curated inner space that I felt proud of. The emotions that I made the conscious decision to hold on to were meaningful and inspired joy and happiness; the ones that didn't were no longer sitting around as a constant reminder of people, situations, and events that no longer fit. Just like cleaning the house isn't always fun, cleaning and clearing out my feelings wasn't always fun either. But I sure did feel good after the fact, and I found that I could breathe in more deeply, just like a freshly scrubbed house makes you want to take a deep inhale of the pristine, citrusy air.

Now that I had the space to feel into my heart, I began to notice that if I changed my behavior, I could heal patterns I'd been repeating, patterns that had kept my heart blocked and my emotions at bay. If I could move the couch away from the wall, I could make the whole living room feel brighter and freer. If I moved that feeling of density from around my heart by changing my habit of pressing it down and shutting it off, then I could feel lighter and more open. Now there was space for new things to arrive, and it felt as if I myself was opening and blossoming. For me, this meant opening up to a new identity and new ideas and clearing the way for the true version of me to reemerge like I did with my childhood box. I distinctly remember my parents remarking during that period, "It's like we got the old Elaine back." Of course, I wasn't suddenly 12 again, but what I *had* done was pave the way for my true nature to reemerge, and that felt freeing and exciting. It felt like giving myself permission to explore a newer and truer version of myself.

Visualization for the Heart

Just like the heart pumps physically, your chest cavity pulsates energetically. Our aim here is to bring that energetic pulsation into a calm and steady rhythm, much like the beating of your physical heart. To begin, tap gently on both of your clavicle bones to draw your energy to this area of your body. After several taps, place your hands over your heart and connect to your breath. (I'll share a specific practice you can use for this, a calm, steady technique I call "Anywhere Breath," later in this chapter.) Visualize the deep love that is lying there, right under your hands. As you feel your heart energy calm, open your palms to face upward, as if releasing your hold of any stuck energy around your heart. Imagine clearing this area so it's pristine and feels as light as a feather. Place your hands back onto your heart, imagining only love and pure light shining inside your heart and chest. Give gratitude to the divine that wants to heal your tired heart and bring in its radiant healing energy.

Space to Shift

I think that most people tend to underestimate the importance of their environment, when, in fact, having a handle on our space is deeply important to our overall well-being. When I was unhappily married, my environment was completely out of control. Living like that made me feel stuck and directionless. It disconnected me from myself and made it difficult for me to feel like I had ownership over my life or my joy.

Once my environment was under my control, when I took ownership of the energy I surrounded myself with, I was able to see things in a different way. Today I'm very protective of my environment and attentive to how I can set it up in a way that feels soothing and relaxing to me. This is certainly true in my home, and it's also true when I'm away from home, wherever I happen to be spending my time. When I'm feeling out of control in my life, one of the first places I look to is my environment—what shifts can I make in my surroundings to change my energy? This includes physical items, but, again, it's more than that: it also includes things like scents and sounds and the energy of the people who I'm sharing space with. How can I offer my senses the refresh they crave? For example, if I'm in a restaurant where the music feels too loud, I might redirect my senses to intentionally focus on the flavors on my plate and appreciate how they delight and nourish me. If I find that I'm getting sucked in by the digital world and my body is reacting with a feeling of anxiety and overwhelm, I might make a point of stepping outside into nature so that I can connect with my own humanity—and perhaps that of others as well—and recalibrate myself with the beauty of the natural world. I think author Mary Davis put it best when she wrote, "A walk in nature walks the soul back home." In a more urban environment where nature's not so readily available, I might walk around and make a point of smiling at and connecting with others and noticing how it makes me feel when someone smiles in return, holds a door open, or extends some other gesture of kindness.

It's also helpful to bring nature into your home. Bring in things that remind you of your natural environment and your connection to it—live potted plants, natural woods, stones, and crystals. Open up the windows or design the room so that your eye is drawn to them, allowing you to take in the beauty of the land that surrounds you.

When your environment is in a state that feels right and comforting, your heart can settle, your stress will begin to dissipate, and you'll find that you experience a greater sense of relaxation and ease. If you pay attention, you might notice that your entire chest softens as you settle into a place that feels aligned with the state of mind you want to be in, where the energy is clear and flowing. The effect of this is profound but often underrated. I first felt this in my previous work as a dental hygienist when I noticed how the entire feeling of the small rooms I was working in were impacted by a patient's energy and that the energy didn't necessarily leave along with the patient. When I felt dense, stuck energy, I started to move and clear it simply by using my hands to, for example, brush away the energy left behind in a dental chair and out of the room (this looks similar to smudging, but without the sage stick). I noticed how the room felt noticeably fresher and lighter for the next patient when I did this and how it set them up for success rather than immediately dragging them into any lingering energy the previous patient had left behind.

By the time I got into my coaching work, I was very familiar with this connection between environment and state of being, but I quickly realized that it isn't something most people consider. I started teaching my clients how to identify and clear stuck energy in their home, place of work, or anywhere else they spent their time. I've seen people who have cleared the stuck energy in their environment suddenly sell houses that have been on the market for months, get a vision of the direction they need to take next in life, find new jobs, and so much more. To me it's abundantly apparent that this is because our environment is an extension of ourselves and vice versa.

My client Lisa came to me because she was feeling dissatis-fied. From the outside looking in, it seemed like Lisa's life was great! She had a sweet relationship with her happy and healthy 14-year-old daughter, was fulfilled by her work as an artist both financially and creatively, and had a close group of friends. She was well aware that she had it better in life than most, but it still felt like something was missing. Lisa felt stagnant in a way that she couldn't quite define, and at times, she also felt overwhelmed.

Lisa came to me because of this sense of stagnancy and over-whelm, and as our conversations went on, she admitted that she craved a romantic partner. To Lisa, these seemed like two sepa-rate issues, but I suspected that they were actually intricately related. As Lisa and I spoke, I tried to ask her to get to the root of her overwhelm, but, as is the case for many people, it felt all-encompassing and difficult to explain. She usually replied that she felt overwhelmed "with it all" as she waved her hands in the air. And there's no doubt that Lisa had a lot on her plate as a working mom with a healthy social life. After a few sessions, I asked her specifically about how she felt in her home. We had done a couple of video calls by this point, and I noticed that there appeared to be a picture of Lisa and her daughter along with a man in the back-ground. Knowing that Lisa wasn't married or in a relationship, I was curious about who that person was.

"It's my ex-husband," she replied.

Gently, I asked her why she had a picture of someone who she was no longer in a relationship with displayed in her home.

"Well, he's my daughter's dad," she told me.

As our calls went on, it became clear that this picture wasn't the only relic of Lisa's past in her home. For as much as I believe Lisa *was* hanging on to some pictures of her former husband for her daughter, that didn't explain the wedding and engagement rings she still had in her jewelry box, the other trinkets from their relationship stored in her home, or the e-mails and voice mails from him that were still saved on her phone. I noticed that whenever the subject of her ex came up, Lisa brushed it off. "I'm fine," she said time and again before moving the conversation in another direction.

It seemed apparent to me that all of this was connected to Lisa's difficulty in dating, as well as her general sense of feeling stuck in the muck of life. It felt hard for her to find the time to date, and when she did go out with a man, they rarely made it to a second date, despite what was obviously her very genuine desire for touch, intimacy, deep conversations, commitment, and emotional support.

Once I had earned Lisa's trust, I suggested that perhaps keeping her past so close at hand in her home was preventing her from moving forward in life. I told her I thought it would be helpful to go through her physical environment one piece at a time to try to shift the energy of stagnancy and make room for new energy to come in. I watched her stiffen at the thought, though it was also clear that she was struck by the idea that maybe she *was* holding on to the past more than she'd been admitting to herself. Finally, she told me, "That feels scary."

"I know it feels that way," I replied. "But I really do think it will help."

Closing her eyes, Lisa nodded. "We can try it," she agreed.

I asked Lisa to start by removing one item from her home that reminded her of her ex. Seeing her start to panic, I assured her, "It doesn't have to be significant or particularly meaningful—just one thing. Let's just pretend there's only this one item to take care of. Just this one. This is the only thing you need to think about."

Lisa began by deleting one voice mail from her ex that she'd been saving on her phone. When we discussed how she felt about it the next week, she told me, "It was hard to do, but I actually felt relieved once it was off my screen." On her own accord, she deleted the other voice mails she'd been saving from him while we spoke. Week by week, Lisa got rid of one thing after another that reminded her of her ex—pictures, notes, jewelry, mementos. After a while I didn't have to prompt her. I noticed that she was suddenly much more open and vulnerable in discussing how the end of her relationship had hurt her and how protective she felt about her own heart, not to mention her daughter's. Sometimes she cried when we spoke, other times she was angry, and sometimes she shared her hopes for the future. Each time we met, Lisa seemed a little bit lighter.

By the time we were done, Lisa had swept through her entire home, leaving just one picture of her ex placed on her daughter's nightstand: a picture of her daughter with her dad, together without Lisa.

A few months ago, I received an invitation to Lisa's upcoming wedding. The invitation she sketched by hand includes not only Lisa's and her fiancé's name, but also her daughter's as they celebrate their growing family together. When I reached out to Lisa to congratulate her, there was a vibrancy to her voice I'd never heard before. "Thank you for helping me let go so that I could move on," she said. "I didn't even realize I was doing it."

Lisa and I are certainly not the only two people who have ever built a wall around our hearts. In fact, it's a pretty common experience. Sometimes the pain and energy of *feeling* and processing just seems like too much. But if we don't feel, we can't heal. And if we don't have access to our hearts, we don't have access to *ourselves*. If we allow ourselves to feel our emotions, they actually come and go quickly, almost like a wave coming into shore and flowing back out again. It's through caging those waves that they build up power and force, like a large volume of water pressing up against a dam.

Living Open-Hearted

It might sound silly, but that matinee showing of *It's Complicated* changed the scope of my life and was my first step back to myself after years of building up walls around my heart. It felt good to feel again, because feeling felt like me. Which is not to say the feelings themselves felt good, because they didn't. The entire reason I had shut down in the first place was because I wanted to avoid the pain that I knew would come from being vulnerable enough to feel.

Each emotion I felt cracked another piece of the shell I'd built around my heart. I wasn't only feeling my own pain, either. The more that shell cracked away and the more I allowed myself to feel into my own experience, the more I felt other people's pain as well, because my own vulnerability also unlocked compassion to a degree I had never experienced before. This was true on a larger level, and it was also true in my own home. I found that the more I felt—and thus could move through—my own pain, the more I could help my children through theirs. I'd thought I was already doing that, but now it was on a deeper level. The more I could feel their pain, the more I could help them move through what they were going through to get to the light. And we did, together— even though it wasn't always easy. Every difficult feeling that I felt, that we felt, allowed me to gain more confidence and understand that it was *okay* to feel and that it was only by feeling the difficult things that we could move through them to another place, to alchemize the pain of emotion into something different. But it was very much like walking through a storm without an umbrella.

As the months and then years went by and I watched my boys heal, I could see that I was doing a good job and that I could move through difficult times without shutting off the sometimes-painful feelings that came with them. Deciding to be present for tough emotions is a choice. I know that I've certainly made the choice not to face my emotions in the past, and I've seen a lot of my clients do the same.

Instead of moving through the storm while feeling the brunt of the blistering wind, they divert their attention, they try to reroute, to refocus their attention, as if ignoring the pain for long enough will make it go away. This might mean burying themselves in work, excessive shopping, overeating, getting cosmetic procedures done, or even just telling themselves and everyone else that "everything's fine." There are so many ways to numb out to avoid pain, but the problem is this doesn't *resolve* the pain or allow you to process it so that you can move through it. Instead, you just remain oblivious and detached from the good stuff too, since we can't pick and choose which emotions to feel and which to block.

If you're closing your heart to feeling the hard stuff, it means you're also closing it off to the beautiful stuff, to all of the wisdom, connection, and excitement that life has to offer. When I ended my marriage, it felt as though I had lost everything. Everything about my environment changed: where I lived, who I felt I was, my path, all of it. I shut off because it all felt too painful. What I didn't yet understand is that it's by being aware of what doesn't feel comfortable that we ultimately heal and adjust and create beauty. The kind of beauty that opens us up and resonates the most deeply. It's by being awake and feeling into what's not working that we are given the information to shift and make changes to what does. To create a life we feel truly excited and energized about. It's not to say that it's always a simple process, but it's a process that works and that's available to each and every one of us.

Beauty is the antidote to suffering, and when you seek out and acknowledge the beauty all around you in big and small ways, you have engaged in a cycle where you are constantly allowing yourself to clean and clear so that your channel can remain open, receptive, and resilient. Notice when the sun hits your face. Notice how you can shift your couch over to the left a little bit more so that you can glimpse the greenery outside every time you walk through your living room. Look for the beauty that's all around you in every moment of every day if only you're open to receiving it. The more you see and feel this beauty, the more you will embody it, and the more you will vibrate at the highest level.

Your Environment Talks to You

Since your physical space soaks in your energy, it can prompt you to notice when your internal environment needs your attention. I've found that not only are people's homes mirrors, but so too is the environment surrounding them, which usually means their yard. This is particularly true as we get deeper into this work and have cleared the residual energy from around our heart. We've done the deep cleaning, so now we can more easily notice when spring cleaning needs to happen. Our environment can not only show us when this clearing needs to take place, but it can also help us intuit exactly what it is that we need to address. Obviously, this is an art and not a science, but that's one of the reasons why getting quiet is so important—so that we can notice those things that may not otherwise be immediately obvious or readable.

About a year after my now-fiancé, Michael, and I moved in together, I noticed that something was off about one of the two beautiful hibiscus bushes that grew alongside one another in our backyard: it looked as if a palm tree had seeded itself in one of the bushes and started to grow. Now it seemed that the palm was in the process of taking over, sucking away all of the water and sunshine that the hibiscus needed to bloom and grow. Meanwhile, the neighboring hibiscus remained vibrant with beautiful green leaves and red flowers. I'd never had a problem with those bushes in the nine years I'd lived in the house up to that point, and I always looked forward to this time of year when they burst into bloom. Both of these bushes received the exact same amount of water and sunshine, and yet one of them was thriving and the other was not. I knew that if this continued, the hurting hibiscus would ultimately wither away.

As I looked at those hibiscus bushes and noticed the pain I felt thinking about the undernourished one, I realized that they were reflecting something happening in my own life that I had yet to acknowledge: for as much as I loved Michael, ever since he'd moved in, I felt as if the energy I needed to thrive had been sucked out of me and reallocated to him. I needed my own unlimited source of water and sunshine so that I could thrive on my own without being overtaken and withering away, giving my own precious resources to someone else.

To be clear, Michael's and my relationship was healthy in so many ways, which is why I believe it took the hibiscus for me to see what was happening in my life. It felt good to let love into my heart again and to be with a partner who stood by me. And yet, at the same time, I was ignoring my longing for independence. I didn't know how to act in a healthy relationship since I hadn't been in one before. Michael wasn't actually doing anything wrong—he was just receiving what I was offering. The problem is that I was giving too much. I didn't know when to stop and wasn't in the habit of being honest about my own dreams and desires—with either myself or my partner. It hit me hard, this feeling that I had lost myself in a relationship *again* without even realizing what was happening.

Much like the chaos in Lisa's environment reflected her feelings of being overwhelmed by the past, mine reflected the ways in which I felt stifled and drained. And while I understand that it may sound like I was reading an awful lot into a wilting hibiscus, because I had done the work of moving energy around my heart by this point, I was able to clearly hear what my heart wanted and needed me to know.

Just as I had to pull the palm out of the garden to save the hibiscus so that it could come back to life, I also had to weed out the behaviors in my and Michael's relationship that were holding me back. I had to stop showing up in this still-new relationship as my representative rather than as myself (something that I find many of my clients do in their desire to be loved). I had to cultivate confidence in my true self and learn to believe that Michael would love me even when I wasn't agreeable or presenting myself in the shiny way that a representative does. I had to make sure that I was remaining true to myself in any and every situation he and I encountered and not giving away anything that I didn't have the resources to offer. I got clear about my primary values and made sure that each decision I made put those values into action. I realized that, for me, personal freedom and self-acceptance were primary values, and yet I'd never put those into action in any of my romantic relationships before.

Ultimately, Michael served as a mirror that allowed me to see those energies I needed to shift in my life to be a truer version of myself. While making these shifts in my relationship wasn't easy, I'm so glad I did. It felt like it represented a huge energy shift, not only in my relationship with Michael, but also in myself and my relationship with God and the universe.

I'm happy to say that this newfound confidence and caretaking of myself has lasted to this day. I have learned that I have a partner who will hold space for my truth without judgment, and I have also learned that I have the ability to understand which energies in my life need to be shifted, as well as the power to create those changes.

Breathe and Beat with the Universe

Over time I released the vise grip on my heart that had kept me from feeling anything in my effort to stay "safe" and, instead, did the opposite: I surrendered it. I now understood that what I once thought of as protecting myself was actually hiding—hiding myself and the truth of who I was—and that I could no longer do that. The price was simply too great.

To be vulnerable is to be courageous, and it is the only way to fully live. When you're vulnerable you're open to all the love in the world. When you're vulnerable you release the pain of loss instead of resisting (and thus holding on to the pain). And, of course, this means you must first *feel* the pain so you can transmute it.

In my own life, I came to realize that I had a lot of pain to process. I had to clear out and heal my judgments of others, my anger, and my sadness. I had to clear out all of those old negative beliefs I'd been holding on to for so long. I had to allow this process to happen, to get rid of the old so that there was room for the new, just as I had made room in my closet and my cupboards. I had to clear out these old repetitive feelings, thoughts, conversations, and patterns so that new, healthier ones could emerge.

And yes, momentarily that hurts, but as we let that pain flow out, the channels also open for the light to flow in—including the breath of God as we allow Him entry and He begins to breathe in sync with the rhythm of our own heart, where He can meet us. As I familiarized myself with this sensation of support far beyond myself, I termed it *Anywhere Breath*. I could take this breath with me anywhere, into any situation, and I would be supported. I no longer had to worry about blocking out the world, because I knew that I was never facing anything alone, even the most difficult situations. This understanding represented a huge shift and a massive opening for me.

Your Anywhere Breath will allow you to feel all of that beautiful open space in your chest. Once you really *feel* that vast expanse, you will want to fill it only with things that are pure and life-giving. You will understand how tight and constricted you were before.

This Anywhere Breath is accessible to each and every one of us, and it's a key to bringing the universe's support in, to connecting our beating heart with its own. But most of us block this connection without even realizing it. We breathe shallowly, keeping our breath close in to protect our heart. This happens unconsciously and probably feels normal—but it's not. It's just a familiar habit. When we hold our breath close to our heart, we are effectively putting up a shield, trying to protect our heart from the environment, blocking everything out and allowing nothing in. To connect with this breath, take in deep, full inhales that fill your belly all the way to your chest and then release it fully back out into the world. As you do this, really *listen* to the sound of your breath. Acknowledge it for keeping you alive and being with you at all times, in all places. Imagine matching your breath with God's breath. Do this again and again.

With my Anywhere Breath, supported by God, I now had a safe internal environment. I could be open and free, I could love people for who they were and let them love me for who I was, knowing that I was in control of my state of being and environment, and could shift them when I needed to. I could shift the emotions inside of me when I needed to, simply by letting them follow their natural course. After everything I'd been through, my heart was stronger, healthier, and more open than ever, beating its strong rhythm in my chest.

When we think of the heart, we usually think of love. And yes, our heart does have to be open and clear to call in and recognize the kind of love that we want to bring into our lives. But the heart also does so much more than that. When you are vibrating with that energy of openness, you are able to draw all sorts of things to you and into your life: creativity, brilliance, ease, a sense of peace, and so much more. When you clear the energy around it, you have access to wholeness and personal truth.

And yet there's a juxtaposition here. I'd wanted to take my sons to Israel since they were little so that we could experience the power of some of the holiest sites on the planet together. We finally had the opportunity when my sons were in their 20s. As we stood in awe before the Western Wall (the last remaining exterior wall of the ancient Jewish temple and the most sacred site of all to the Jewish people), I began channeling messages. I had channeled before, but these messages felt different, almost as if they origi- nated from far beyond the most infinite reaches of the universe. They were also coming in faster and clearer than any messages I'd ever heard before. One that impacted me the most was this: *Your heart is not your own. Your heart is from and ruled by God.* What this means is that each of our hearts is a channel, a direct private line between you and God. When it's clear, you're opening up that channel for God to flow through you with His healing energy or whatever else is meant for your heart. Your heart is the place in you where you surrender your energy to God or the universe. And you cannot surrender if your heart is surrounded by walls or residue. You can't feel the signs that the universe is sending you flutter in your chest or vibrate throughout your nervous system. You can't have the emotional healing that's available to you if that heart of yours is blocked off and inaccessible.

Also, when you surrender your heart to God, He can connect with you to assist you in healing. There is what seems to be a contradiction here. We want to control our hearts, to keep them locked up and safe, invulnerable to pain. But when we do this, we cannot heal. You must clear the channel and surrender your con- trol to God so that He can hold you and do His healing work on your behalf. To give Him this access, though, you must clear the clutter that blocks the way for this healing energy to present itself.

ONCE YOUR MIND IS FREE,

YOU CAN LET IT RUN WILD

OUT INTO THE INFINITE. IN

A STATE OF RELAXATION,

PRAYER, AND STILLNESS,

YOU AND YOUR CLEAR

MIND BECOME A PURE

WHITE CANVAS READY

TO BE PAINTED UPON.

CHAPTER FIVE

GET PRESENT

Clear the Path to Inner Peace

Life can be found only in the present moment.
If we are not truly ourselves, fully in the
present moment, we miss everything.

— THICH NHAT HANH, BUDDHIST MONK

Walking the Labyrinth

Free your mind.

Not coincidentally, path 1, the path of the mind (represented by our head region), is located on the outermost ring of the labyrinth. It is the path that is most exposed to the outer world, and it is also the longest. As we walk this path, we seek to quiet our busy mind, to empty it of all the noisy clutter that keeps us in our head and out of our body and soul and settle into the moment at hand so that we can live a more imaginative, playful, and meaningful life.

Early on in my spiritual journey, I decided to go to an event where esteemed spiritual thought leaders and authors like Marianne Williamson, Deepak Chopra, and Don Miguel Ruiz were slated to appear. I was so excited to be there, and also so overwhelmed. This was still such a new world for me, and I felt like I was learning a language that had been hidden from me up to this point.

As I was walking through a hallway of the conference space, I found myself face-to-face with Don Miguel Ruiz, author of the best-selling book *The Four Agreements*. I had read it along with the rest of the country, and as soon as I finished the *Agreements*, I dove into another of his books, *The Mastery of Love*, because I was hungry for more. Shocked and somewhat in awe, I introduced myself, and Ruiz reached out to shake my hand. As our palms met, I felt overcome by his energy, which I can describe as nothing other than complete and total presence. I had never experienced anything like it before, and the sensation of just being *around* that kind of energy shook me to my core. It was clear to me that he knew something I didn't—and I desperately wanted to find out what that was. I wanted to be so present in my own life, so completely in my power and purpose, so connected with both myself and everyone and everything, that the air around me seemed to shift on a molecular level like it did with him. Yes, I know this is a lot to take away from a brief handshake, but Ruiz communicated *all* of that simply through his presence.

Up to that point, I didn't understand that being truly present changes everything and opens the door to a kind of magic. But by being around Ruiz for even those brief seconds, it was abundantly clear to me that it did. And if I could just get present—really, deeply present—everything else would change too.

Walking the Path of the Head

Just outside of the labyrinth is the hustle and bustle of the world. It's alive with nature, creatures, interesting people, profound relationships, and all that makes up life's precious moments. But remember that, for now, you are here inside the labyrinth, doing the work that is meant just for you. Here there is separation, and the time and space for you to let everything else go so that you can focus solely on quieting and connecting with yourself. This path and the work you do here is how you will learn to live well, both within yourself and out in the world. It's how you will clear the channels to hear beyond the physical world and learn to fully engage in the joy that's out there while also doing the healing, growing, and transformation that your soul yearns for. There is a pull to the outer world, and to all of the connections and stories that are associated with it, but now is the time to quiet your mind, to fight the pull and be here now.

Each path we're discussing in this book has its own challenges, but in my experience, walking the path of the mind can be the most complex of all. Our minds are so busy and the world is so loud, constantly stuffing us with all kinds of new information, that most of us have no idea how to quiet it all so that we can get intimate with ourselves. We never slow down enough to create space for the answers to land, and yet we wonder why our relationships struggle, our lives feel dissatisfying, and we feel disconnected from anything greater than ourselves. The best that most of us experience are brief moments—flashes, really—of remembering that we can access that inner knowing and guidance that our mind drowns out the other 99.9 percent of the time. And so we are left feeling completely lost and disassociated. The constant chatter of our mind is drowning out the important information that we actually need, and it's pulling us out of this precious moment. If only we can get to a place where the mind is utterly still—a skill that the vast majority of people simply don't possess at this moment in history—we can actually drop into our lives, which is where we're meant to be. It's why we're here, after all!

It's impossible to be in the moment when the mind is constantly bouncing from one place and person to another, from the past to the present to the future, from our responsibilities to our concerns to our desires. Our mind rationalizes things, and it makes up stories that can lead us down the path away from presence. The mind rambles incessantly, building up energy as it goes, like the internal version of a person who talks and talks incessantly, almost as if they can't stop. It is the place where reactivity lives. I don't have to tell you how difficult it is to wrangle in the mind, particularly in a world where you're pulled in a million different directions at once. Not only that, but society encourages the mind while downplaying the heart and the soul. We are encouraged to be cerebral beings and are judged by how intelligent and articulate we are, functions that come directly from our mind. Meanwhile, emotions are considered inferior to thoughts at best and, in some cases, even weak.

The intention of this path is to become aware of this chatter and how detrimental it is, so that we can instead make the choice to develop and connect with an energy of presence. Our life force energy exists in the present moment, and if we are not in the moment we're missing out on the power that has been gifted to us in this lifetime. This essential life force doesn't think, it just *is*, and the more we can align with that state of being, the closer we are to our true nature. Despite its constant presence, this deep, most wise and soulful part of ourselves is difficult to connect with over the chatter of the mind.

When the mind runs wild, we are also missing out on all of that divine support we have access to. Yes, the divine and all of your angels and guides are always with you, but their voices are easily drowned out or misinterpreted by your mind. If you can clear your mind, you can really begin to hear and feel their guidance of support.

When you can just *be*—in your body, in your heart, and in the present moment—it's possible to replace the heaviness that often comes with life into lightness. When you're not worrying about the past or the future but simply being in the present moment, it's much easier to recognize that your life and presence are miracles. *You* are a miracle, and that miracle has nothing to do with your busy mind or your to-do list. Your entire purpose here is your presence.

The path of the mind is one of the most challenging, not only due to the nature of how the mind works, but also because of the state of the world. It's hard not to notice that the world is increasingly fast, increasingly connected, and increasingly machine-driven—and it seems to be speeding up more and more at an increasing rate. Busy-ness lives in our mind, and working on slowing your mind in this particular era requires you to walk a path that most others are not.

Busy-ness is the great curse of our time. So many people are disconnected from their higher power, trading humanity for business profits, and living in their head rather than in their heart and soul. Everything is about going faster, and faster is not always better, particularly when it comes to the mind. It's like getting into a car with a driver who's going too fast and swerving all over the road in an effort to shave a few minutes off the ride time. The potential cost is high, and it comes at the price of your nervous system. It's all too easy to get swept up in this material world. And yet, on some level, most of us know it's not the path, and this is precisely why meditation, organic food, massage, yoga, and anything else that has to do with creating harmony in the system and self-care has taken off. People feel desperate to find ways to stay human and not be co-opted into the modern-day digital reality. Intuitively, we are fighting for our very existence.

It makes me so sad when I hear women, in particular, talking corporate-speak like robots, and this is at the root of so much of what we're addressing in this chapter. It's almost as if our *minds*—which have always liked to chatter throughout the course of humankind—have now started to mimic the lightning-speed pace and robotic cadence of the digital world. It's like we're trying to process our own lives in the way technology is processed. The world is moving faster and faster, but we humans are not meant to move this fast. The outer world is developing much faster than our inner world, which is why we must get quiet and focus on what's inside. We are not robots or computers. We are souls encased in bodies, and right now our minds are fighting this world. I can't tell you how many of my clients talk about the experience of "not being able to keep up." Of course they can't keep up with the pace of modern life! They're not meant to. And yet that can feel like a failure in this day and age if you're basing your success on societal or corporate expectations. Despite the state of the world, your mind was not meant to live this high-octane life, and it wasn't meant to process information like a computer. It's no wonder our minds are spinning and we're living in a constant state of exhaustion. We're trying to compete with machines, and it's a destructive, losing battle. While everyone and everything else is going faster, your work here is to go slower, disengage from your devices, and engage with the world.

Another root cause of busy-ness is a sense of not-enoughness, which so many of my clients experience. They want to feel worthy and valued, so they send themselves on overdrive trying to do that, which only results in a constantly racing mind and nervous system. It's an easy trap to fall into because there are more than enough things in this world to distract your mind with, to the point of completely missing out on what's important in the present moment. Collect too many of those moments and an entire life can pass you by.

Visualization for the Head

See yourself walking along a dirt path with a bucket of water on top of your head, filled so high that the liquid is spilling over the rim. You can feel that water requiring so much of your attention and weighing heavily on your body. The spillage turns the dirt path around you into mud, making it more difficult to move without slipping. Allow yourself to place the bucket down and then stand again, noticing how much lighter you feel. Now take that bucket and tip it over, allowing all of the thoughts that are filling your mind to wash away along with the water. Pick up the empty bucket and continue walking, noticing how light and free you feel and how you can now concentrate on the road ahead without worrying about your overflowing bucket along the way.

The Stories We Tell Ourselves

Your mind wants to protect you, and in an effort to do this, it's constantly taking in and processing information to apply to future situations. This is an amazing survival mechanism that has kept humans—particularly our long-ago ancestors—safe. But precisely because of this, your mind holds on to heartbreak and devastation, then continues to react to those past hurts in the present day. It wants to do what either kept or could have kept you safe then, even if it's not relevant to the moment at hand. Your mind can also continue reacting to the past even when what's currently happening has no relevance to what came before, simply because it's negatively charged.

My client Paula came to see me because she was convinced that her husband was having an affair. He wasn't, but this affair was the story her mind created based on a pattern of trauma that Paula had experienced in her childhood. When her husband worked out of his home office, he closed the door to block out the noise from the rest of the house. He explained why he was doing this to Paula time and again, and yet every time the door swung shut, she was convinced that her husband was speaking to another woman. And each time the door closed, Paula proceeded to press her ear right up against it. Not once did Paula hear anything nefarious coming through her husband's closed door, but she was still convinced by, and reacting to, the story playing on repeat in her mind.

When Paula came to me she wanted me to buy into this story, to agree with her that there was something in her marriage that needed to be fixed, and to confirm that her husband was responsible for fixing it. It's true that Paula's marriage *had* become rocky, but not for the reasons she was concerned about—not because of another woman. Her marriage was in a difficult spot because her insecurity led her to falsely accuse her husband of things he wasn't doing, to make him feel as though she didn't trust him, when the truth of the matter was he'd done nothing wrong.

Our mind is tightly bound to our survival systems, and I had a feeling that's exactly what was happening with Paula. Regardless of what was actually occurring (or not) behind closed doors, the insecurity and jealousy felt very real to Paula, as if her mind was trying to get her to see something. I asked Paula when she first felt like she needed to hear what was happening on the other side of a closed door. She told me that she had first done this when she was eight years old and her parents closed their bedroom door to talk privately. Growing up, Paula's strict parents expected her to behave perfectly at every moment. Since there wasn't a lot of open communication in her home, Paula never knew exactly where she stood or why—only that she was either perfect or in trouble, with no in-between. The only way Paula could experience a sense of safety was by listening through her parents' door in case the gauntlet was about to come down.

Our work had nothing to do with Paula's marriage. It was a matter of helping the eight-year-old Paula process the emotions she'd experienced during childhood so that she could feel safe, and also of letting Paula's inner child understand that she was an adult now. That her fear was tied to an event in the past, not the present. Together, we processed all of the emotions that Paula had felt as a child so that when the feeling arose again in the present day, she could identify her mind at work, telling stories. Once Paula could see this, she was able to practice intentionally drawing herself into the reality of the present moment.

When you find yourself in a moment of reacting to a story rather than reality, or of living in the past rather than the present, the first thing to do is to create awareness around the behavior. Notice how you react in these moments. Does your heart start racing? Do you find yourself at a loss for words? Do you feel yourself going into flight-fight-or-freeze mode? All of these are cues that you've been negatively charged. This is important to recognize because in order to connect to our truest and deepest self, your nervous system has to be in a calm state.

REWRITE YOUR STORY

Paula is far from alone in living into a reality created in her mind that's based on the past rather than the present. In fact, pretty much all of us do this. Like Paula, we need to disconnect our thoughts from our emotions. Our emotions play an important role in our lives, but when we interweave unprocessed emotions with our thoughts, they create a story. And almost always that story has nothing to do with the reality of a situation or our present-day life.

To help my clients get a fresh perspective on their stories, I have them run through an exercise I will share with you here. As you think through this, I want you to pretend that you are a reporter gathering information about your life. As a journalist, you are not interested in emotions or a prepackaged story, just the facts. It's almost as if you are watching your own life rather than living it. In fact, I want you to write this factual story of your life in the third person—*she* was born in 1983, for example.

Think back to a time in your youth when it was particularly difficult for you to process emotions and experiences in your life. No adults were present who could help you understand the circumstances; instead, you were left to figure it out on your own. When you identify this difficult moment, take a deep Anywhere Breath in and let it slowly out. Then pick up a pen and paper and begin to write about what happened. Remember—just the facts! You might even list the story out in bullet-point form if you prefer.

Once you've finished writing, take another Anywhere Breath and reread your story. Once you've finished, notice how you feel. Is there a new sense of compassion for yourself? For the other people involved? Does the story seem any different now that you're reading about it as if it happened to someone else rather than yourself? How might this new view of your story change the ways in which you see and react to the world moving forward?

You *can* stop this pattern, and the key is to be conscious of it. When you feel yourself being charged into a state of story, take a moment to pause and relax your entire body. Consciously remind yourself that you are in a present, unique moment, not a repeat of something that may have happened to you previously. Know that your mind has not just the ability, but the *tendency* to make up stories based on the past and to skew that story as the present reality. Your mind means no harm, it's just doing what it's meant to do and, likely, repeating a behavior that's been reinforced over the years, whether consciously or not.

After you've noticed yourself slipping out of the present and into a story, you want to interrupt the conversation. It's no different than if you were sitting at a table and someone started to tell a story about your best friend that wasn't true. Chances are, you would step in and refocus the conversation by correcting false stories with actual facts. You're doing the same thing here, only the conversation exists solely within yourself. Do this over and over as many times as it takes, and over time you will notice that your mind begins to shift away from the stories and rewire itself to concentrate instead on the reality of the present moment.

Breathe the Animal Away

We collect pent-up energy in our mind when we allow our thoughts to live there, rambling away. Those thoughts collect and swell until they feel like a big balloon, ready to pop at any moment. Your balloon is filled with your own fear-based or repetitive thoughts, the thoughts others have shared with you, the media you've ingested, and the more general fears of the world. Like a balloon with too much air, you have to release that energy caused by ruminating thoughts. If that air is not released, the balloon eventually morphs into a wild, caged animal, pacing back and forth through your head, building up intensity and ready to strike.

When you encounter this animal, don't show it that you're afraid. Instead, do the opposite of what you probably want to do— which is to relax. Come back to that Anywhere Breath once again and just breathe. Do not engage or make any sudden movements. *Don't react to the animal.* If you do, that mythical creature in your head that's grown and morphed from all of your thoughts will wreak havoc. So instead, just keep breathing. If you relax (or at least simulate relaxation until you actually achieve it), eventually the animal will calm too. At that point, when it's more sedated and has been lulled into an inactive state, you can escort it out of your mind. The next time you hear that animal pacing outside your door, don't open it and allow the animal back in again. Instead, repeat the practice: *stop, relax, breathe slowly and steadily.*

Your breath will act like a release valve to let all of that pent-up energy out of your head. After a while, the animal will realize that it's not getting back in there, and eventually, when it no longer feels your fear, it will wander away once and for all.

And now, without that animal in your mind or outside of your door waiting to get in, things are peaceful. Your mind feels calm, clear, and present. And every now and then, your mind might become so clear, so unclouded by pent-up thoughts, that it even feels as if you have no mind at all. Will that be a constant state? Almost surely not. But even a glimpse of it is a beautiful thing, and it's your own relaxation and deep breaths that hold the key.

Once your mind is clear and you're no longer subjecting your-self to the fear-inducing animal, you have the space to not only think for yourself, but also to hear those thoughts as they arrive, beckoned by reality and your inner voice rather than as a reac-tion to fear. Continue to practice breathing, clearing, and being more selective about the thoughts that are allowed to occupy your mind, and over time, you may find that you're able to make the leap from a clear mind to a no-mind state, where there is no mind as we conceive of it on the human plane, only energy. Reaching this state of being for even a second feels like pure peace, connec-tion, and spontaneous presence.

Once your mind is free, you can let it run wild out into the infinite. In a state of relaxation, prayer, and stillness, you and your clear mind become a pure white canvas ready to be painted upon. There is a swirling collection of information just waiting to present itself to you so that you can bring it forth. Here you have access to the answers to all of the questions you want to ask; you only have to make space for them to enter your consciousness.

This is realized only through relaxation, which we'll delve into more in the next chapter. Once you harness the energy available to you from this no-mind, relaxed state, it will feel like a bolt of lightning courses through you as energy rushes through your body. The physical sensation of receiving this kind of divine energy in the 3D realm can sometimes feel similar to an adrenaline rush, but you want to stay relaxed and calm even through this, relying on your Anywhere Breath to do the trick.

Bringing in information in this way is completely different from anything you've ever experienced in your overthinking mind. There's a clarity to both the information you receive and how you process and receive it that simply doesn't exist in this realm or in information derived from this plane, and it *feels* different. You'll find that focus comes easily in moments like this, and you are flooded with a sense of aliveness—like you can feel life itself coursing through your veins in a way that you are deeply present for and aware of. That's because what you're hearing in this moment are answers from the divine that are meant specifically for you and you alone, because those answers match your brilliance and capacity of understanding. Receiving this information requires only a fleeting moment of a no-mind so clear that it's only energy. When you receive information in this way, listen carefully, almost like a court reporter. Listen to every word and write them down as they're relayed to you, as if your life is at stake. It doesn't matter how you do this; just do it.

From a human perspective, there seems to be a contradiction here: When you experience a moment of profound clarity like this, it comes easily. There is no work involved. And yet after you receive this communication, you will need to rest because it's such an intense surge of energy and state of focus. It's as if your no-mind has ventured out into the vastness of the universe, danced around the galaxies, laughed and cried, and played like a child. All in the space of a fleeting moment.

Once you experience this energy, you will understand that it is always here and available to you. Ask for the experience, and it will arrive.

Living with a Clear Mind

One spring day, I pulled into my driveway after grocery shopping and pressed the button to automatically open the trunk of my car so I could bring the groceries in. Not paying attention, I rounded the back of the car and hit the half-opened trunk full force, right on my hairline. I had been too stuck in my own head to notice that the trunk hadn't opened all the way until my head literally came in contact with it. I was barely able to keep myself standing up straight.

That evening, as I began to fall asleep, I started to clearly hear my guides speak to me. Up to that point in my life, I had been hearing my spirit team, but I wasn't fully committed to believing all I was hearing. Getting knocked out that day, I believe, was their way of gently nudging me toward believing and taking action. I'd always been intuitive, but now downloads were coming in like a tsunami, constantly and clearly, to the point where I couldn't even sleep at night, because so much was coming through and I couldn't bear the thought of going to sleep and missing out on all of these new insights that were available to me.

In retrospect, this story makes me laugh because I literally had to get hit across the head in order to wake up and pay attention to what the universe was trying to tell me. It's as if it created an empty space that spirit could work through. And that's exactly what you're going to do once you put the concepts in this chapter into play in your own life—only in a less literal and physically painful way! We're all built to hear the messages the universe wants to give us.

The universe is here to help you with its wisdom and guidance. Also, *you* are here to bring that guidance into your life and into the world. But first you have to be able to hear what the universe is saying over the constant hum of all of that chatter running through your head. *What is the universal message you can open up to to help humankind?* Because, I assure you, it's there just waiting for you to get quiet enough that you can receive it.

Let go of the stories ruminating around your mind, and release the voices that are putting so much pressure on you and that expect and fear so much. Just being you is enough. You are the only you who will ever grace this planet—what a gift you have been given, and what a gift you are to the world! That's all you have to do and be in this moment.

Your job is nothing more or less than to be here, to be present. You are like a majestic oak tree, here simply for the pleasure and enjoyment of your grand beingness. It's that simple, and making it any more complicated will only result in suffering. When you are fully present in yourself and to the world, it will feel effortless, because that is the one and only thing you were designed to do.

YOU CAN SENSE IN YOUR

GUT, HEART, AND MIND

THAT YOU'RE ON THE

RIGHT PATH. IT'S TIME TO

RECEIVE WHAT YOU ARE

NOW OPEN ENOUGH TO

INVITE INTO YOUR LIFE.

CHAPTER SIX

GET REST

Relax to Receive

Leisure is a valid human activity.

— NATHANIEL BRANDEN, PSYCHOTHERAPIST

Walking the Labyrinth

Create space for rest so that you can refresh and receive.

Now that you have bravely journeyed through the longest and most exposed path of the labyrinth, the path of the mind, it's time to turn inward as we come to path 4, the middle path of the labyrinth. With a clear mind, you come back to this middle space, where it's so much more peaceful and quiet. After all of this work you've done, it's time to recover, rest, and receive. On path 4, we notice the hips, which is where stagnant energy and emotions are stored. It's time to release all of this so that we have room to receive a newly designed vision for our lives.

It was the first time I'd gotten away in years, and I was traveling by myself through a small town in central Mexico called San Miguel de Allende. As the trip neared its end, I felt like a completely different person than I had when I arrived—rested, renewed, and relaxed. I knew that some of this sense of renewal came from simply getting away and having time that was all my own to do what I wanted, with no obligations to anyone other than myself. But, also, there was something about the energy in the town that helped me let go and unwind in a powerful way. San Miguel de Allende was a beautiful place, not only visually, but also energetically. It seemed that artists were drawn there, and the entire town was overflowing with color and creativity. Warm smiles greeted me everywhere I went, and there was a subtle buzz of magic in the air, which made my heart open and my body release. It's as if the uplifting environment had allowed a heavy weight I didn't even know I was carrying to float away.

As I was walking around on one of the last days of the trip, feeling open and free, soaking in the beauty of everything around me (including *myself* and how beautiful I felt in the flowing red dress I wore), I decided to visit a historic 17th-century church called the Parroquia de San Miguel Arcángel. I sat down in a pew to soak in the beauty of the towering domes, sparkling chandeliers, and stained glass, feeling both dwarfed and calmed by its splendor. Just as I was about to get up, people started flooding into the church, all of them dressed up and electrifying the air around us. I realized that a wedding was about to begin, and on a whim, I decided to stay. I watched as the handsome groom came in and stood at the altar, where he greeted his gorgeous bride when she floated down the aisle a few minutes later. I grinned from ear to ear as I watched these strangers promise to love and care for each other for the rest of their lives.

In the precise moment when the officiant married the beautiful couple, I heard a clear voice ring in my head: *You are ready to receive.* It was as if something inside of me broke open, and suddenly it was clear to me that I was going to find love and get married again. This understanding filled me with joy, not just at the idea of sharing my life with a loving partner, but even more so because I understood that it meant I'd healed the heavy energy I'd been carrying around with me and was now able to move my life forward.

I was excited about the idea of calling in my soulmate from this much healthier newfound state of being. I was more connected, more vulnerable, more self-realized. I understood that I couldn't take on the workload I had during my younger years; I had to receive at least as much as I gave. I didn't know exactly what a romantic relationship would look like at this point in my life, but I did know the kind of partner I needed, and I knew that I would be ready to receive him when he came. And sure enough, before long, my now-fiancé, Michael, arrived.

Now it's time for you to receive too. Don't underestimate the deep work you've done up to this point of the book. Even if it's intangible, it's meaningful work—it represents some of the most transformative work you'll do in your life, because you're reconnecting with who you really are and all that you were meant to be when you stand in your own beautiful power. You're halfway there now. You've brought life back into your body, taken care of your precious heart, and done the deep work of clearing your mind and finding your center and peace amid all the noise of the outside world. Here you find yourself in the middle of the labyrinth, far from the perimeter. You still have a way to go before you reach the center, but you can start to taste it now. You can sense in your gut, heart, and mind that you're on the right path.

And now it's time for rest. It's time to receive what you are now open enough to invite into your life.

It's safe to say that one of the things women underestimate most is rest. The effect of this lack of rest is profound: it negatively impacts our personal happiness; our emotional, physical, and mental health; and our spirituality. Most days, you likely run from here to there, exhausted as you begin the day, let alone when you end it. We believe we don't have time for rest or it isn't something we "deserve" without having "earned" it. And when we do earn rest, it's a stolen hour here or a few extenuating days there.

Yes, getting away for an hour or for a few days is great. But make no mistake: it's not enough. Rest on a regular basis and in day-to-day life is nothing short of a necessity. Unfortunately, emphasizing rest feels almost counter-cultural, because we're so driven by the busy-ness we've discussed in previous chapters. Now, with a clearer mind and heart, you're ready for true rest, ready to allow yourself to release and let go in a way that is rejuvenating and empowers you to receive.

Rest is one of the biggest and most underrated ingredients to living your best life. I can't think of a single time I've ever had an epiphany or come to a new understanding when I wasn't in a state of rest—can you? This is not a coincidence. When we're able to rest and relax, we're also able to more easily connect to the subtle energies that support us and are more open to receiving the information they have to share. While we were able to open up to some of this connection in the previous chapter by clearing the mind, this next step of relaxation is vital because when we can both relax *and* have a clear mind, the information flows through more quickly and easily. It allows us to more easily connect with that energy that greets us in the labyrinth—the playful, all-knowing yet innocent infusion of light. So when I'm talking about rest, it's in these terms. Yes, rest requires relaxation, but it's mostly about attuning to the state in which you are able to explore these subtle energies and really listen to and receive the messages they offer and feelings they inspire.

Walking the Path of the Hips

There are few things in this world we underestimate more than rest. People are often skeptical when I tell them that I first began to feel my power through resting, and I would have thought the same thing before experiencing the profound transformation and bliss that rest offers. We live in a culture that places little emphasis on rest and often even judges it as laziness or a lack of drive. Up until I learned how to rest, I often felt agitated and frustrated. Yes, I made progress and started to move to a better place before I incorporated rest into my life, but at this point in my journey *this* was the single thing that changed everything for me. It allowed me to relax into myself, understand the important energy of receiving, and more easily hear myself and the subtle energies of the universe, which offered me clearer direction on the road ahead.

My clients are often surprised when I tell them that an integral—and often overlooked—part of stepping fully into their power is to slow down. Even if they have gathered certain parts of their power, it's not fully available until they learn how to rest. This is the final push to get them beyond that feeling of "stuck" so that they are free to soar and realize both their full potential and that of the universe around them.

To be clear, rest and sleep are not the same thing, and you need both. Rest is a conscious process, whereas sleep is not. Sleep is hard enough to get in the doses we need, but both the modern lifestyle and ethos have moved far enough away from the idea and practice of rest that it's something most of us have to relearn. Rest is natural and something that we require to be healthy human beings from a holistic perspective. This state of awake relaxation offers a chance for the body and soul to consciously mingle and play together.

The first—and often most difficult—step of rest is giving yourself permission to do so. You—yes, you—deserve and require rest. Every single day. And not only do you need to rest, but you also deserve to *enjoy* resting, to prioritize it. It's important that you give yourself permission to rest, but if you're not yet there at this moment, please know that *I* give you permission.

Granting oneself this permission usually requires a change in mindset. Consider the fact that what you've been taught about making progress in life and in your relationship with yourself and the universe isn't actually about constantly pushing forward at all. Maybe instead it's through *stopping* that you move forward. And I don't mean stopping for a moment's break here or an extra hour in bed there. I'm talking about building the equivalent of a cocoon around yourself, your own private space where it's safe and warm and cozy and just for you, and then returning to that cocoon on a regular basis. Here in this cozy cocoon, you can fully let go and relax in order to prepare for the next stage of your growth and evolution. The only thing being asked of you here is to rest and transform—no forcing is required.

It's so quiet in this cocoon. There are no distractions, and there is nothing to attend to. I bet you'll be surprised to find that things are happening even as you rest. You are growing and understanding new things about yourself and about the world. All of this silence allows you to hear in a way that hasn't been possible until now. Rest gives you a necessary opportunity to savor all of that presence you generated in the previous chapter and to begin to live and be grounded in this beautiful being that is you. It's an opportunity to hear all of the inner guidance without all of the noise of daily life. It will help you soak in all of the magic that's found in the subtleties of life so that you can relax into your brilliance.

If you don't choose rest, chances are that sooner or later it will find its way to you, though perhaps not in a way you might prefer. This happened to my client Natalie. Natalie is a mother of three elementary school–aged children and a well-known architect, speaker, and author. She had always struggled to say no to any requests or opportunities that came her way, whether they were professional or personal. She'd reached a point of burnout and her marriage was in bad shape when she became gravely ill from an autoimmune disease and nearly died of liver failure. Forced to rest, she spent five long months on the couch recovering. During this time, her friends and co-workers were very supportive.

Two years later, Natalie had recovered her physical health but knew she was on the verge of burning out again, and her marriage was in even worse shape than it had been before. The difference was that this time Natalie understood that she was playing with fire. She decided to choose rest before rest chose her this time, and she knew that she needed space to figure out what needed to change in her life. She was also aware that she would need some significant time and space to recharge, so she booked two weeks away from her family, work, and friends in the shadows of Camelback Mountain in Arizona. Natalie knew that she was doing what she had to do for her health and to gain some perspective, but that didn't mean her decision was easy. Leaving her children was difficult, and she also feared that people would judge her for doing so.

When Natalie first arrived in the apartment she'd rented, she unpacked, then sat down at her laptop to structure out the weeks ahead. This worked for a few days, but the more Natalie fell into a slower, more restful pace, the more she realized she didn't need a routine. Next she realized she didn't need her cell phone with her at all times. Then she started doing the things she *wanted* to do instead of the things she felt she *should* do. For a while, her inner critic chattered away, but Natalie silenced it by firmly telling that voice that she needed a break.

After a few days of this, Natalie found herself crying uncontrollably one day, seemingly out of nowhere. The tears continued to come for an hour as Natalie sat on a lounge chair releasing decades of pent-up emotion, realizing that life could be different than how she'd been living it all this time. She understood in a way she hadn't before that it was possible to live a life that felt good to her rather than one that other people deemed acceptable or appropriate and that required her to spend the vast majority of her time giving and running. When Natalie returned from her time away and filled me in on her experience, she explained that the answers she'd found weren't cognitive—they came from a deeper level. By removing herself from her day-to-day routine, it became crystal clear to her how unhealthy and, frankly, insane it was that she only acknowledged her need to rest when she arrived at death's doorstep. She could clearly see that she'd built a prison around herself for years, and now she was ready to build rest and space into her life to free herself from those bars.

I'm happy to say that today Natalie's life looks much different than it once did. She had the strength to leave her marriage and now revels in her own space, which she shares with her children. Her work has changed quite a bit, too. Before, she had a big platform and consulted with big brands on highly visible projects.

When Natalie slowed down, she realized that what made her heart sing was the architectural work itself, not the accolades that came with big-name projects. She pared down her work, only takes on projects she loves, and actually *feels* powerful for the first time ever, professionally. Best of all, she's the picture of health. She ensures that rest is built into her life, and that includes time set aside for a walk and mindfulness practice every day. She prioritizes allowing herself to slow down so she can hear herself think, no matter who she lets down in the process. She frequently visits Arizona so that she can reconnect with the desert, an environment that makes her feel grounded and at peace with herself and the world around her.

There is no right or wrong way to rest (though hopefully it doesn't look like the collapse it initially did for Natalie and isn't charged by a life-or-death event). The only thing that matters is that it works for you. Rest might involve getting away in a very literal sense, but we can all work in moments of rest throughout our day, and that will look different for each of us. Rest might look like a warm bath with Epsom salt or some quiet time spent in nature. It might mean journaling or taking some time just to breathe. It could be bodywork or professional stress management. It might mean reading, gardening, or going to a place that makes you feel happy, like the ocean or mountains. It might be hiking, forest bathing, skiing, or boating—something that appears active but soothes your soul and quiets your mind and body. It might be spending time with your family (though not in a way that asks you to be the facilitator).

You can also weave these restful moments into your daily routine. When you speak, clean, or listen, you have an opportunity to relax into the present moment. When you groom your pet, fold your laundry, wash the dishes, or pick out your clothing for the day, you can make a practice of releasing your worries and inviting in peace. In doing this, you are making a conscious decision to welcome in an experience of peaceful, restful flow. You are getting yourself into a receptive state on a regular basis.

Rest is a state of mind, and it can come with you anywhere and into any situation.

Visualization for the Hips

Imagine the stored energy of pent-up emotions in your hips tangled up like two knotted balls of yarn, with one ball in each cup of your hips. See yourself gently pulling on each ball of yarn, pulling and pulling until there's nothing left to pull. Once the yarn is out of your hips, watch it disappear into the air. Place one hand on each hip and notice how spacious they feel now without those tangled balls. Send love directly into each hip as you focus on breathing into them.

Learning to Receive

Only once you rest can you truly understand how to receive, because the two go hand in hand. When you show yourself care and nurturing, you will start to soften into self-love and compassion toward both yourself and others. Although we don't often think of it this way in the Western world, Buddhism views rest as an act of compassion, because when we are well, we're better equipped to help others. What you feel, the world will reflect back to you, offering you what you know you deserve. Just like we will never reach our full potential without rest, we will also never reach it without learning to receive. Before I knew how to rest, I also didn't know how to receive, for many reasons both cultural and personal. I gave in my relationships, I gave at home, and I gave in my work. Yes, these never-ending acts of perpetual giving were a choice on the surface, though they didn't necessarily feel like that. From a young age, society tells girls that they are nurturers and givers, but it has little to say about receiving.

As little girls, we're taught to be polite and selfless. The belief is instilled either subliminally or overtly that we'll get what we want by embodying these qualities, that we'll be thought of as "good." As we age, we're given the role of nurturers and caretakers. And yes, many of us want and even savor this role. But that doesn't mean we're meant to give, give, give at our own expense until we're left with a dry well. Excuse my language, but that's complete bullshit.

What can actually happen when you live in this way is that, in addition to never learning to receive, you may also very well attract people to you who are takers, creating a toxic cycle of deeply unbalanced giving and receiving. When you find yourself in this difficult situation—whether it's because you don't know how to receive, because you've drawn takers toward you, or some combination of the two—you will end up feeling depleted, as if there's nothing left for you. Resentment and exhaustion start to set in. Giving, which can be a lovely feeling when it's done out of choice and from the heart, starts to feel like a duty, almost as if you're doing it despite your will.

After 20 years of this, I felt angry and resentful. I was tired of giving far beyond the extent of what I had to give and, all too often, feeling as if I didn't even have a choice in what, when, or to whom I gave. I sat with this feeling and was suddenly struck with the realization that some people *were* offering me things as well. I just didn't know how to receive them, so the scales remained unbalanced. *What would happen if I gave myself permission to receive the support that people were offering me?* I wondered. This felt like a novel, almost revolutionary idea. I understood that since I wasn't used to receiving, I would have to develop the capacity, just like any new habit.

Like me, most women aren't taught much about receiving. Because we don't know how to receive ourselves, we can also have the tendency to judge others for doing so: *Why is she taking time off when her family needs her? That woman seems so lazy. I can't believe her husband does all of the cleaning!* I know I used to make these kinds of judgments. I used to judge friends for taking time out for self-care or receiving in any way, because the idea was so foreign to me. *That's not what moms do . . . right?* Of course, none of this is true, but because rest goes against the culture and rest requires receiving, we create a self-perpetuating cycle.

I now understand the true power of receiving and how desperately we need to practice this skill. It's possible to give and give and give until we're sick (often quite literally) and tired to the point where we're out of our minds. Receiving is just as important, and it's a *practice*. Quite the opposite of being lazy, when we receive, we're saying to the universe, *I honor you, I see what you've created, and I acknowledge that you put me here to experience it all.*

To receive, we must surrender, which requires a conscious choice. We are choosing to release what's beyond our control and receive whatever is meant for us. When we really do this, we can relax. This requires breaking a lot of habits that have been built into many of us throughout our lifetime, including: giving at all costs, way beyond what we actually have the capacity to offer; orchestrating everything and everyone around us; and people pleasing.

When we receive, we feel a greater sense of connection to this world where everything can feel so separate. Separate is scary— it's not relatable, which means it's not safe. But when we're connected, we feel free. We understand on a new level that we are all interconnected, and in this connection and oneness is safety. We can release so much fear when we realize that we are not alone in our experience and the world. No matter how different our experiences might be, we are all souls from the same place, living out this human experience at the same time.

As I practiced receiving, I realized there was an energy to it, an entire direction of flow that I'd been missing out on up to this point. Because I knew how to give but not to receive, it meant that all this time, energy had been flowing in only one direction: away from me. It's almost like there was a clog in the pipe. The energy that I scattered everywhere wasn't being replenished because I was deflecting the nourishment of various forms that flowed my way. Once I allowed myself to begin receiving this energy, I also understood that I was worthy of it. From there, I began practicing the next step, which was to proactively *ask* for what I needed. Michael was a great way for me to dip my toe into these waters. I started by asking for simple things, like help lifting something heavy out of the car or picking up something from the store. Yes, these are small tasks, but as a single mom who was used to doing everything, they felt huge to me. It turned out that every time I asked Michael for a favor or expressed a need, it made *him* feel good too, because it demonstrated that I trusted and needed him. For so many of my younger years, I thought that I needed financial support from a man, but it turns out I needed someone to honor my heart. After practicing asking and receiving at home, I began to take this new skill out into the world by asking for what I needed from friends, in business situations, and sometimes even just out in the world of day-to-day situations. Most of the time, people were happy to oblige; when they couldn't, they explained why. As I built this practice, a weight of resentment that I hadn't even known I'd been carrying around lifted—the weight of feeling like I was somehow responsible for doing everything if it was going to be done right. It turned out that simply wasn't true!

As that energy started to flow in both directions like a dam was lifted, I experienced a huge release I had no clue I needed. Anger, fear, and sadness all came pouring out of me. For as much work as I'd done processing and releasing unfelt emotion around my heart, I realized through this experience that there was an entirely different level of tension, grief, and fear that I'd been holding on to deep inside of me. It seemed that, unlike the emotion I'd held around my heart, this emotion wasn't so much for me to feel but to release—and I couldn't do that until I felt relaxed and safe in the understanding that I could ask for what I needed. My clients have experienced a similar release. The sudden rush of all these emotions that we don't even know we have hidden away inside of our bodies can feel shocking, but it's also freeing. Once all of that residue is out, a new freedom and lightness sets in, and a new level of relaxation in the body and soul is possible.

If you, like me, haven't made a habit of receiving—and perhaps either consciously or subconsciously don't even believe that you're worthy of it—remember that both giving and receiving are actions of love, which means they are intricately related, and that the energy behind both of these actions is important. Now think of all the things you give and all of the people you give to, and ask yourself why you give to them. What is your motivation? Are you giving because you want to or because you want to please someone or keep the peace? How does it feel to give? Do you feel depleted or resentful? When we give with the expectation that someone will give us something back or love us as a result, the energy of that giving becomes impure or imbalanced, which can result in feelings of depletion and desperation. Now think about what prevents you from receiving. Is it fear of intimacy or connection? A feeling that you somehow don't deserve it? If you feel any of these things, consider who you are potentially receiving from and if you want to be in an energy exchange with that person. If the answer is yes, remember that you are built to both give and receive, and that the energy of both flow equally from a state of pure generosity.

Giving and receiving are a way of not only expressing and aligning with the energy of love you have for others, but also the love you have for yourself. Once I started to receive from others, I realized that I could also receive from myself. Most often, I found that what I needed was rest and relaxation, time and space for me alone. For me this meant taking walks by myself at night and hanging a door hanger on my bedroom door that read "Getting Quiet" and then closing the door behind me. I went deep into self-care like acupuncture and massage and incorporated them into my regular routine (which felt frighteningly extravagant at first, but I've now come to see these practices as essential). In the stillness that came from rest and rejuvenation, I could hear and feel into myself better. Now I was no longer waiting until I was exhausted to drop. Instead, I was making a conscious decision to give myself the gift of rest—whatever that looked like on any given day. In that stillness, I could feel self-love and a new life force building up inside me. The force was subtle enough that I was largely unaware of it until I stopped to rest and turn inward.

We spend so much time racing around, thinking that we're going to somehow fill ourselves up in the process, when really, it's through stopping that we begin to feel whole and filled up. In the course of true, deep rest, we have to relax and receive. That might mean receiving the sounds of the environment around you as you swing in a hammock outside, soaking nature in with your defenses down. It might mean saying yes to a favor someone offers you so that you can have time to yourself, relieved of responsibility, releasing control in the process and receiving their kindness. It might mean receiving the messages and epiphanies that come in these moments of relaxation and understanding the connection between you and the universal powers assisting and guiding you. When we have enough of these moments of relaxation and then experience the receiving and sense of connectedness that come with it, the entire world takes on a new color, and we bring this same awareness into our more active moments as well. When we rest, we are gathering up the energy we need to receive all that the labyrinth has to offer us as we approach its inner paths. Because this energy bubbles quietly beneath the surface, it can be easy to miss, but we access it when we rest.

One of the greatest compliments I've ever received was from a masseuse. At the end of our bodywork session, she looked at me with tears in her eyes and said, "I love it when people are able to fully receive." This meant so much to me because it was a reminder of how far I'd come—from someone who only knew how to give beyond what I actually had to offer to a person who was able to trust, surrender, and receive.

Shift into Neutrality

Beyond the logistics of finding time for rest in a busy world, rest can also feel intimidating for those who are resistant to understanding who they really are or confronting their inner demons. But the truth is there's nothing to fear. Yes, it's true that you may encounter thoughts and emotions that feel difficult in the midst of rest. Know they are there for a reason, and that reason is so that you can identify, process, and clear them. The kind of self-understanding that's gleaned from this will allow you to settle into your personal power so that you can shine your light even brighter. Being you to your fullest, which means embracing both shadow and light, is your birthright, and it's important to honor that dance.

Rest itself provides you with the tools you need to overcome these and other fears, because it allows you to shift your energy into a state of neutrality, where your fears and anxieties stop running the show. But first, you must acknowledge those uncomfortable feelings. The next time you feel agitated or fear rises up, write out a list of all your fears in that moment, just as we did in the previous chapter. Specifically focus on what you worry is going to happen in the future. Getting it out of your head and onto a piece of paper will remove the chatter from your mind and help your system relax and quiet. As you read back over your fears and frustrations, you might even realize that they aren't realistic when you see them written out in black and white. Now that those thoughts are out, rest into your Anywhere Breath, and then offer yourself whatever you need to relax, and come back to a neutral state.

While this exercise will help you in the moment, I recommend taking it a step further to alleviate pent-up fear and worry in a more long-term way. This is important, because these are the types of emotions that become lodged in the hips, ultimately creating both physical and spiritual tension and blockage. We associate carrying the weight of the world on our shoulders, but really we're carrying it down here in the cups of our hips, where it blocks our ability to move through life with a sense of fluidity. To begin, write today's date on the same piece of paper where you've listed your fears, and tuck it away somewhere you won't lose it. Revisit that list when the situation you were worried about has resolved itself or at a certain point in time down the line (I like to review these lists once a year). Chances are you will find that none of these fears manifested—or if they did, it's likely that either you were capable of handling them or that the reality wasn't as bad as you were worried it would be. This practice allows you the opportunity to show your nervous system that it's okay, and to release the residue of any fear and anxiety you've been carrying rather than holding on to them over time and allowing the associated emotions to store up in your body. Also, working these feelings out of your body will allow you to settle into a more restful state on a day-to-day basis and reduce the likelihood of energy getting trapped in the future.

As you know by now, the more relaxed you become, the easier you will be able to access the information that's trying to come through for you. This relaxed state will support your clear mind, allowing you to more easily connect with and hear the energy of the divine. In those clear hips, you are able to access the more subtle energies, like angels and guides. Angels are the energy of those who have passed that you might have known in this earthbound state and are now helping you from the Other Side. Your guides may or may not have been earthbound, and you may or may not have known them at some point. You might have one or you might have 20. You can think of your guides as a professor in college whom you didn't know well but learned a lot from.

Like all of our spiritual helpers, these entities are not forceful in nature, but they want to connect with you. In fact, I would go so far as to say they *desperately* want to connect with you, to show you the way and teach you. Their wisdom and insights will always be gentle, never nagging, and will only come when you tap in and meet them halfway. As soon as you're ready to do your part—which involves clearing stuck energy and sinking into a state of relaxation—know that they're just waiting to connect with you, waiting for you to ask about the pressing questions that are weighing on your heart so that they can gift you the answers. They will find you in this space where you are open, your inner universe is quiet, where the energy is calm and conscious.

Savor the sense of inner peace that rest bestows upon you. Of anything you can receive, this is the most priceless gift of all. The best part is that it's a gift you can give yourself—more easily than you might think! By creating time and space for yourself to do whatever it is that settles you and aligning with the energy of receiving, you will transform not only yourself, but also the world around you. When you find peace within, you will emanate that out into the world, spreading that energy to others and opening yourself up to an entirely new world of possibilities. Instead of feeling as if you are always fighting with and against the world, now you are open to seeing (and receiving) all of the beauty and goodness it's offering.

PART III

DISCOVERING

THERE ARE STILL MORE

PATHS AHEAD OF YOU TO

WALK, BUT NOW YOU CAN

SEE WHERE YOU'RE HEADED,

AND THE JOURNEY IS MUCH

CLEARER THAN IT HAS

EVER BEEN BEFORE.

CHAPTER SEVEN

GET GROUNDED

Know What's True for You

Forget not that the earth delights to feel your bare feet and the winds long to play with your hair.

— KAHLIL GIBRAN, WRITER AND POET

Walking the Labyrinth

Clear old patterns and beliefs and get grounded in a new way of moving through the world.

You've relaxed and restored, and now it's time to move forward on path 7, which is associated with your feet. You're now just two paths away from the center of the labyrinth, so close that you can feel the energy of that center point emanating out and casting its powerful energy upon you. You can catch a glimpse of your dreams that are safely stored just up ahead and also glance behind you to see how far you've traveled to get to this point. You can use all of that information from both where you're headed and where you've been as you walk this short but powerful path. With each step, you feel infused with clarity and focus, because you can now see where the path is leading you.

I came to a point in my journey where I realized that I would never go back to living the life I had been living before. Yes, some elements of it might remain the same, but my state of being had permanently shifted, which changed the way I saw the world and everything in it. It changed the way I saw *myself*. All of the work I'd done had resulted in a newfound sense of self-love bubbling up, and that changed everything, because my standards for what I wanted and deserved transformed entirely. It changed how I interacted with myself and with the world, how I made decisions, and the way in which I wanted to live my daily life. While my life might look much the same as it had before to people on the outside looking in, it *felt* like a whole new world to me.

I no longer felt beholden to anyone or anything that didn't make me feel how I wanted to feel, which was supported and nurtured. I could both receive people into my life and also know that I was okay by myself. I only allowed people who valued me and whom I valued in return into my inner circle. I was no longer willing to give my power away. I was discerning about my time and energy and made sure that I fiercely protected both for things that mattered to me, for things I chose to do, and that I also allowed myself some time to just be with me—whatever that meant on a given day. I didn't dither over decisions or feel stuck anymore. I knew I could handle whatever came my way and that I had power over what my life looked like. I felt confident that I would honor myself along the way rather than focusing on giving this energy away to others.

I think of it like coming to a point in the road where I encountered a bridge; once I walked over that bridge, it crumbled behind me, and there was no looking back. Whereas this might have felt scary before, now it felt invigorating and profoundly right. I had outgrown the old path. I didn't want to go back, and it felt like a surge of energy was propelling me forward.

If it feels like all of this happened quickly, that's because it did. There was the inner work that came before, yes, but once it all settled—once I was in my body, had freed my heart, cleared my mind, and allowed myself to exist in a more relaxed state—I had primed my body, heart, mind, and soul for grounding in this new way. From that new state of being, I experienced a quickening in my personal evolution.

As we step onto path 7, you are no longer shifting energy in the ways we have been up to this point in the book. In the previous paths, you were removing energy blockages so that your energy could flow more freely and start to dance with higher vibrational energies. Now you are connecting more deeply to and working with those powers and forces that your misaligned energy was previously muting, blocking, and dimming. You now have the ability to recognize and then clear fearful energy as it arises and live out your soul's mission. Yes, there are still more paths ahead of you to walk, but now you can see where you're headed, and the journey is much clearer than it has ever been before. Because you have done so much processing, healing, and growing, you are now able to engage with your life in a way that hasn't been possible in a long time—or perhaps even ever before. You have a new *knowing* about you that guides the way and a recognition that you do, in fact, have a soul's mission. Even if you don't know precisely what that divine calling is yet, you know that it's there, and you're getting glimpses of it along the way!

Grounding into Your Path

It's time to shift your attention down to your feet, which move you forward and ground you down to earth, this place where you've come to experience humanity and fulfill your purpose in this lifetime. You arrive here with a new sense of lightness thanks to all of the energy you've shifted and heaviness you've shed. While what we'll discuss in this chapter might have felt aspirational or even impossible at earlier stages, now it will feel oddly simple. Not only that, but you have recently discovered a sense of harmony with all of these energy channels flowing so freely through you. Whereas you've been *working* up to this point, now you are settling into *being*. It's likely that moments of inspiration are arriving unbeckoned and you're able to capture those moments with a sense of clarity and ease that you haven't experienced before—or at least not in a very long time. In these moments you hear the call of your soul leading you toward your purpose in this lifetime, planting seeds of inspiration and insight along the way. You are an open and clear vessel for God and the universe to work through; because you've discovered this openness and clarity, the collaboration and support that were always available to you now feel tangible and accessible. What you previously couldn't hear is now loud and clear in the quiet you've cultivated throughout your being.

In the past few chapters, we've been discussing new ideas, perspectives, and ways of being to blend into your life, and now you will harness all of that energy and begin to ground your life in all of this newfound knowledge, wisdom, and understanding. It's time to take all of those discoveries, revelations, and transformations and use them to shift your state of being (for example, shifting from sadness to happiness or from meekness to confidence), and you will realize this by shifting your focus. Here, your focus will move away from those things you've been distracted by for so long—your obligations, unhealthy relationships that aren't working, the old stories that you have about yourself—and relax into what's true to you.

With this clean canvas you've cultivated by letting go of residual emotions and quieting your chattering mind, you get to start fresh and clear, free from the emotional and mental weight you've been carrying. Not only that, but now you have the benefit of a crisp connection to tap into those energetic sources that can help guide you toward the area of focus that's the most resonant with you and feels the truest to your soul. All of this allows you to experience a new form of grounding in your own life and your own truth.

When we talk about grounding, it's usually from the perspective of grounding down to the earth. And yes, we are doing that in this chapter. But that's only half of it. You've probably heard the word *grounding* before in the context of tethering ourselves to the physical plane, the reality you're living in. To me, this definition of grounding implies stagnancy. I want to be very clear that this isn't the goal of this chapter at all. I believe we've gotten the concept of grounding all wrong, which has led us down the wrong path. When I think of grounding as it's usually conveyed, I imagine roots growing beneath me and going in one direction, which is down, where they continue to grow, building hundreds of networks underground in the dark, where the sun cannot penetrate. It reminds me of the many women I've encountered who have planted figurative seeds in their lives without being thoughtful or intentional about what will take root as a result—this might be a job, marriage, or home that ends up holding them down to a place where they don't necessarily want to stay, entrapping them in decisions they've made and versions of themselves they cannot move beyond.

As divine souls in embodied form, we are grounded to the earth, yes, but we are also inextricably connected to the heavens. Rather than roots, picture a brilliant, fluid, and wide ray of light beaming out of you in two directions: up toward the sky and down into the earth. That glorious ray of light is divine energy moving through you, and there's nothing that can block those beautiful rays because they're so bright. The light illuminates what's below and holds you both up and down, while still allowing you to move and shift as necessary. Even before this point, when you couldn't necessarily feel or sense those rays flowing through you, they were always there because they are your divine birthright. And now that you *can* understand and sense them, their impact is profound. That light comes out of the bottoms of your feet, attaching you to this earth and grounding you to the path you're meant to walk. It also shoots up in a straight line from your ankle creases, brushing against your body all the way up to your frontal lobe (which governs higher cognitive functions like personality, problem solving, memory, and emotions) and up to the heavens above. This light running through you allows for a co-creation between you, heaven, and earth.

Walking the Path of the Feet

By this point, you have generated the power and connection to access unexplored potential and capabilities that you may have never before recognized in yourself. Along with this may come a new vision for your future to imagine and propel you forward. As you begin to better understand your truth—who you are, why you're here, and where you're heading—you can use all of that information and inspiration as a grounding force to provide you with a new direction in life. You move more quickly now, with more confidence and a lighter state of being. Without all of the excessive burden you were carrying before, there is less distraction and a new sense of momentum and personal growth. You have a sense of what is actually true and meaningful to you rather than the distractions or inherited patterns that may have been driving your path or sense of identity up to this point. It feels joyful and affirming to move forward with this kind of transparency and intent. You can likely feel that you're getting closer to something, even if you don't know quite what that is yet.

With this grounding energy you've generated comes a new sense of stability and oneness that firmly connects you to the earth. It's the same kind of stability that plants and trees must feel but that has eluded many of us humans for most of our lives—a sense of safety in knowing that we are nurtured and at home here on earth. It's like an energy exchange between you and the earth, and the melding of those energies through your grounded feet is designed to hold, power, and nourish you when you most need it. This kind of stability brings with it a new sense of serenity, because it means that you always have exactly what you need, no matter how hard the wind is blowing. Best of all, this stabilizing energy is available to you at any time, anywhere you go.

A sense of being supported and nurtured is important. Feeling at one with this earth and understanding that you are nature yourself, with a distinct role to play and mission to fulfill, is important. But so is movement and the ability to shift your state and focus as you learn and discover new things and have access to increased depths and layers of inner wisdom. You are meant to live in a state of spontaneous presence that supports you in remaining true to yourself and focused, unwavering in whatever you might encounter, and able to embrace it all.

At the same time, the grounding light that moves upward brings with it a sense of quickening and lightness, which holds you up and keeps you connected to the place where your soul originated. How nonintuitive that grounding could come from above—but it *is* both above and below, connecting your heavenly soul to this earthly plane, with both sides guiding you and cheering you on as you move forward.

Once you become aware of and can feel this energy, it's even more simple to shift your focus and your state. That light that extends up to your forehead radiates out some more, gathering information so that you can discern in an instant what is right for you and what is not. What needs to leave your energy field and what needs to be protected? What thoughts and emotions are serving you and which are not? All of these senses and all of this support work together to create a quickening effect. Things that once felt difficult now feel free, flowing, and sometimes even instantaneous. Whereas you were once confused and blocked, now you are armed with the power of innate awareness and knowing. In this state, with this guidance and empowerment, all it takes is one new insight, one new shift in perception, to see your life in a new and profound way, and to confidently adapt accordingly. All of the questioning and worry that used to consume so much of your energy are replaced with unshakable inner wisdom. Answers, experiences, and people who are meant for you arrive more quickly because that bright unfettered light that's running through you sends a beacon out to the world, drawing what you focus on toward you, moving you closer to your purpose and your purpose closer to you.

It's true that even here, life will not always be perfect or easy; after all, you are still living an embodied human experience. Every now and then, you might still falter or lose your way. But you've made it far enough that when you *do* step off the path you want to walk—when you lose your way or your state of being slips into a lower vibration—you will be able to feel it. You've experienced this sense of grounding in your new life path, and the path will call out to you in those moments when you might stray from it.

One of the most joyful parts of my work is witnessing clients as they round this bend of their journey. When it arrives, it's like watching a missing piece click into place. One of my favorite examples of this happened with my client Clara. She was entrenched in the technology industry, but everything about Clara was the opposite of corporate. Anytime the topic of her job came up during our time together, it was like all of the life drained out of her. But she lit up from head to toe when we talked about her travels with a group of marine biologists on expeditions to tag whales so they could learn about how they migrated and birthed their babies.

I pointed this distinct difference out to Clara several times, but she waved it away. She didn't feel like she knew enough to make a sustainable living through environmental work. But over time, as Clara worked through the Get Quiet Way, I saw her begin to shift and become more open to new ideas and the possibilities ahead of her. I could tell that she was beginning to sense that her true calling was marine life. Once Clara accepted the fact that the ocean was what really called to her and focused on creating a life around that, her energy shifted and it was clear that she had a new divinely guided inspiration. After that, the logistics came quickly in the form of an environmental position that was perfectly suited to her background. A newly invigorated Clara explained to me that before she'd been working a job; now she was living a passion. Not only that, but her fears of not being able to sustain herself turned out not to be true.

Like Clara, many people fear that shifting their focus will upend their lives in ways they're not prepared for. What if their true life calling doesn't seem to offer sustenance or might require a significant shift in lifestyle? I'm not advocating for you to tear down your life or create hardship. But I *am* advocating for you to listen to where you feel called and acknowledge how allowing yourself to hear that call feels and how it changes you, because these nudges and flashes of inspiration and knowing are never without reason. Often, abundance follows even if you don't initially know what that's going to look like. Don't underestimate the importance of financial security; I've found that when women can create a foundation of financial stability for themselves, they're able to be completely honest about how they want to move through their lives, to follow their passion, and to choose people and partners who they are aligned with. In other words, they can stay true to themselves.

Sometimes a path that you wouldn't have imagined possible seems to present itself out of nowhere; other times, you might shift your existing career in a way you hadn't thought of or feel newly invigorated by what you're already doing as the result of a different focus or state of being. There's always room for expansion, whatever that looks like. And there's a good chance you don't know what that will or could look like until you reach this point of grounding.

But also remember that on this path of the feet, the emphasis is on changing your focus and state. This may mean that, for example, when you decide you're worth more, the universe will start opening doors. My client Anna is a perfect example of this. Like Clara, Anna worked in corporate America. She liked her work enough, but she didn't like the feeling of being stuck, and she'd been in limbo for quite some time. She was waiting for her good work and the significant amount of time she'd invested with her company to be recognized with a promotion, waiting for colleagues to leave or retire so that she could step into their position. The waiting didn't feel good to Anna, but she felt like she had to because she had invested a lot of time in the company and was making a lot of money, and it felt scary to give up everything she'd worked for. People frequently end up in situations like Anna's, where they're making enough money that they settle for a life that isn't really meant for them.

Anna dreamed of having her own executive coaching business and training up-and-coming leaders, but she was afraid to make the leap. As we walked the labyrinth Anna clearly heard

It's go time. She told me that she'd heard this message many times before from various therapists, coaches, and inspirational books, but there was something different, more powerful and resonant, when she received this message in the labyrinth. She felt in her bones that the message was coming from a much deeper source. After walking the labyrinth, Anna set her intention to find a way into this niche she felt called to. In my opinion, she did the hardest work of all in that session by *making the decision that felt most true to who she was and what she wanted.* In doing this, Anna reset her focus and state of being. I often find that when a person makes this conscious shift in energy—when they decide on the path they're going to walk—things start to happen, as if there's some sort of magnetic force at work. Sure enough, a couple of weeks later, I got an excited message from Anna that she'd been invited to speak to a global leadership group. As she spoke at that conference, she was able to step back and hear herself speak out loud for the first time. Through that, she finally fully recognized her own knowledge and expertise for the first time, and her confidence and sense of value increased as a result. With this, Anna understood that she was done being in a situation where anyone else determined her value or timeline. The very next day, she gave her employer two weeks' notice and made the leap. Very quickly (we're talking within weeks) she built a coaching business that went on to impact hundreds of people—at each step along the way, it felt like she was guided and working from a state of ease and flow.

Anna is a great example of the quickening effect of this path. She had all of this bottled-up knowledge and wisdom that she hadn't yet decided to unleash. Once her direction was clear, once Anna decided where she was going, she had the confidence, momentum, and support it took to bring her vision into reality. When this happens it's like a snowball effect, because courageous acts build confidence and we're propelled forward with a powerful energy. Five years later, not only is Anna's coaching career continuing to flourish, but she's also become a serial entrepreneur to the extent that I've lost count of how many businesses she has her hands in. Gone is that sense of limitation that once held Anna back. Today she embodies a sense of personal freedom and confidence, and it gives me great joy to watch her soar and have the time of her life doing it. Her energy is light and bright, and it's very clear that Anna is doing exactly what she was always meant to do—no waiting required.

Visualization for the Feet

Visualize yourself looking down at your feet and noticing huge rays of light shining out from the creases of both of your ankles, radiating out in front of you and lighting the path ahead. The light also extends up, brushing against your forehead and continuing all the way up to the heavens, as far as you can see. You feel the bottoms of your feet, solid, strong, and connected to the ground underneath you. As you walk forward, casting this light above and ahead, you look down and notice that your feet leave imprints of light behind you, lighting the path for others to see and follow.

Getting Loud

Somewhat ironically, considering that this book is about quieting various aspects of ourselves, once women reach this point of their journey, it's as if they suddenly find their voice. This doesn't happen in an aggressive way (because that would involve changing your state or focus and giving too much of your energy away), but once you shift to this clear and grounded place, it feels almost impossible to remain quiet when something is abrasive to your soul. It's as if your belief system has been rerouted, and there's no longer the arduous grind of trying to figure out how to work through situations in the way you're "supposed" to or that will maintain a certain appearance.

Instead you understand quickly what works for you and what doesn't, and you have the ability to express that without an undue measure of overthinking. It no longer feels okay when someone isn't valuing or honoring you at the highest level, and you can put voice to that. This comes as the result of understanding the truth of what you're worth and what is and isn't okay, then feeling safe to express that in the moment. This is great news, because the one way in which women generally *are* too quiet is when it comes to speaking up for themselves.

Now you will find it easier to speak up and stand in your power, to protect your energy when someone tries to dim it, dictate it, or take it away. This doesn't mean arguing or shifting your energy in any way that feels negative to you. When you understand what you will and won't accept for yourself, it becomes possible to handle situations clearly and without hesitation, but also with grace, because you will not give away your energy in the process. These situations can arise in both big and small ways. It might mean kindly but firmly telling your partner what you really need when perhaps you haven't felt empowered or comfortable enough to do so before, or holding a line or boundary with your kids without slipping into anger or frustration. You can do this knowing that you have the right to stand up for what you believe and want, big or small, and that doing so doesn't have to invoke fear or be somehow off-putting to the other people involved. You are claiming your feminine superpower when you exude the confident, wise, intuitive, and sure-footed energy that is divinely gifted to you at birth.

AS MUCH AS YOU MAY

HAVE STUMBLED AND

FELT TOSSED AROUND

BEFORE, HERE YOU ARE ON

A PATH OF GRACE, JOY, AND

INNER PEACE. YOUR PATH

WANTS YOU TO WALK IT.

CHAPTER EIGHT

GET EXCITED

Move Your Dreams Forward

It is precisely the possibility of realizing a dream that makes life interesting.

— PAULO COELHO, AUTHOR

Walking the Labyrinth

Understand and embody your passion and purpose, and know the steps to take to get there.

You have now arrived at path 6 of the labyrinth. The energy of this path is associated with the legs and, specifically, with the thigh and the kneecap, which are respectively the strongest parts of your leg and the parts that offer you mobility to move forward and walk the path ahead. You move forward to what you know is meant for you and precisely what you came here to do.

In my own journey through the Get Quiet Way, I couldn't help but notice that the deeper I walked into the labyrinth, the bigger and better the opportunities presented to me became. By the time I reached path 6, I could feel energy coursing through me. I felt strong, alive, boundless, purposeful, and peaceful. I felt fulfilled both by what I had already accomplished and what I knew with every fiber of my being was still ahead. I was overflowing with gratitude both to have made it to this point and in knowing that there was more to come. In so many ways, this was just the beginning. The future no longer felt daunting, but instead seemed like a buried treasure I had finally found and was ready to bring to the surface. Best of all, I was truly appreciating *myself* for the first time in my life.

The only problem was that there was a part of myself I had given away before. And now it suddenly felt vital to get that part of myself back.

By this point I had been divorced for 10 years, and my life looked completely different than it once had. I had raised two young men who were kind, smart, and focused on their own passions, created a purpose-driven business helping people along their life paths, and committed my heart to a loving and kind man.

And yet I had done all of this under a name that wasn't my own, almost like I was living my life under an alias. Despite all that I'd taken action on, I still hadn't yet legally changed my married name back to my maiden name, the name given to me at birth. I felt conflicted once I reached this place where I wanted nothing more than to be the fullest version of myself possible. All the shifting and healing had led me to remember exactly who Elaine Glass was and to see her clearly and in her purest form. She was so lovely, beautiful, and sunny. She was empathetic and loved big, she was patient and safe. I was headed toward my purpose and I knew with my entire being that all of Elaine deserved to be along for the ride and claim that journey.

For years I didn't go back to my maiden name because I wanted my last name to be the same as my sons'. It felt like I was somehow abandoning them by leaving the name we shared behind, and that was the last thing I wanted to do. Still, I couldn't ignore the fact that it suddenly felt critical to attach my own name to this life I'd built and was so proud to be living. I was moving forward and expanding, and yet there was this one element of my life that felt as though it continued to tie me to the past every time I signed, said, or saw my name. Finally, it got to the point where I had to approach my sons to have a conversation about this. I spoke to them both individually and, although it was a change for all of us, they understood. It was impossible not to tear up and feel over- whelmed with pride when they each told me in their own way that no matter what my name was, I would always be their mom.

When the day finally came to change my name back to Elaine Glass, I happened to glance up as I was filling out the necessary paperwork at the government office. Across the room from me I saw a couple who looked so much like my grandparents that I did a double take. In that moment, I was hit by the emotion of it all, thinking of all my ancestors, many of whom had passed. I was struck by how the change I was making felt like a restoration and reclamation of a legacy, a name that would live on in the world. It felt like honoring them by allowing my family's last name to live on, and it felt like they were honoring me by sharing this name.

It wasn't until my name officially legally reverted to Glass that I fully realized how much our names are intricately woven in every little facet of life. I had to change 15 years' worth of databases where my name was registered: at the bank and on credit cards, on my e-mail account, at the grocery store, and, of course, at the dreaded DMV. While changing the name on my driver's license, I suddenly became aware of the song playing on the sound system, "Fame," from the movie of the same name (one of my all-time favorites). I tuned in right as the lyric "Baby, remember my name" played. I smiled to myself, knowing that this and all of the other synchronicities I was noticing at that point in my life were little nods from the universe affirming my new identity and reassuring me that I was heading in exactly the right direction. Every time I made a powerful decision that led me to a document where I had to sign my name, I was reminded of how good and important it felt to be wholly myself. I was reminded of who I was and what

I had accomplished every time I made an investment in myself, provided something for my family, or signed on to a new project that worked toward fulfilling my passion and purpose.

Finally, I returned to myself, the only version I truly could be or wanted to be. By that point, I hadn't seen Elaine Glass since I was 28 years old; so much had happened since that time. At long last, I felt free to merge who I had been with who I had become and to move forward from there. While it's true that there was a lot of pain around no longer sharing a last name with my sons, I was able to remain confident in my decision because it also felt very much as if I'd finally removed a suit of armor that I hadn't fully realized had been weighing me down. Now I felt free to continue walking the path that led me away from my old stories and toward new and exciting opportunities. I laughed out loud when I visited a numerologist shortly thereafter who told me that Elaine Glass corresponds to "healer, counselor, teacher" in numerological terms. I should also mention that my married name in numerology meant "manifester," so that version of Elaine did serve me—I manifested so much during those years, which got me to a point where I was willing to live the life I wanted to live, the life of my dreams, as the truest version of myself.

In your own way, you are now ready to move your dreams forward as the truest version of yourself, whatever that means for you. Now that you've grounded down with energy flowing through you from the heavens up above and down into the earth, new realizations, perspectives, and continued healing are flowing freely through the open channel you've created. With that comes a new sense of confidence and direction that will allow you to walk boldly forward to whatever it is you're dreaming of, waiting for you just up ahead.

These legs of yours have been sprinting along toward elusive goals for so long, toward other people's expectations and dreams. Now it's time to power yourself toward your own dreams. At long last, you're ready to move toward *your* dreams and to uncover the treasure that has been buried within you. You sense a feeling of lightness that's been missing up to this point, and even in the moments when it's not easy, you can feel your legs firmly under you, nimble and agile as you move toward your dreams.

The Power of Purpose

Take your dreams seriously, because they represent your purpose, which I define as your soul's energy organized and realized on the human plane. The pure energy from a place beyond this world is calling you to express and live those dreams out here on earth. At this point, your bigger purpose is rising to the surface, presenting itself to you and calling you forward. Often that purpose presents itself in the form of dreams, both those that come to you while you sleep and those that you play a more active role in as you let your mind wander. Through these dreams, your soul gives you a taste of what it most deeply desires, and now that you can hear that calling loud and clear, it's up to you to continue moving toward all of your visions. Your path is free of obstacles and you gather momentum and forward movement with your destination in clear view. This movement feels exciting, and you are powered by the motivation of fulfilling your dreams.

This sense of purpose is generally accompanied by a greater sense of self-love: you understand why you are here, what you came here to do, and how your journey so far—both the easy and the difficult parts—has led you to this point. Finally, you understand that you are headed in a direction more in alignment with your soul. You're curious about and excited to see what comes next, with a newfound sense of trust in both yourself and the universe that you are moving toward, embodying all that you came here to be and do. You are now starting to see how and why your purpose matters not only to you, but also to the world. As theologian Frederick Buechner puts it, "The place God calls you to is the place where your deep gladness and the world's deep hunger meet." The reason why we experience such unhappiness when we don't understand our purpose is because our soul knows that it's not living out its destiny—and it's also why we can experience such deep happiness once we do identify that purpose and allow ourselves to fully commit to and dream in that direction. Women are the keepers of the soul. We are not in our natural state when we're disconnected from our higher self and cannot hear it speak.

It's also important to understand that you may have more than one purpose in this lifetime; in fact, you may have many. Continuing to chase an old purpose after it's been lived out will no longer leave you overflowing with excitement, light, and a sense of fulfillment, so be present to what you're feeling drawn to. Allow yourself to be open when you feel the call from within, even if it means changing directions. Give yourself permission to change and evolve in this lifetime. Stay awake to new energy, feel and acknowledge what moves you, and trust that it's okay to change. After all, you were built to evolve and expand—that's why you came here.

If you find yourself feeling unsure about your purpose, ask, *What brings me joy and fulfillment? What are my unique talents and strengths? What issues or causes do I feel deeply about? What would I do if I had unlimited resources? How do I envision my ideal future? Who do I admire and why?* Trust that the answer will present itself.

With this sense of purpose, you will find and understand yourself in a way and to a depth that you've never known before. It might even feel as if you have a new identity. As you dive deep to understand this identity, you can think of yourself as a scientist, curious and experimental, asking questions and testing things out. This contemplation and discovery should feel playful because that's the energy of your soul, and it's the energy that has the ability to connect you with your brilliance. Frustration and fear have no role to play as you draw closer to your purpose. There's no such thing as "taking too long" or doing things "the wrong way." Experimentation is part of the fun, so trust and follow your urges, even if they don't seem to make any logical sense. As I was walking the labyrinth one day, I heard: *Be brave. Listen and learn.* With that message in mind, I decided I wanted to do something that was out of my comfort zone each and every month for the rest of the year, even if it didn't seem to fulfill a specific purpose. I wanted to do things that challenged and even scared me. I started off with Toastmasters, an organization where participants learn and practice public speaking skills in a community environment. Not coincidentally, public speaking is my greatest fear, so I figured I might as well jump right in! While the actual speaking was a sort of out-of-body experience, I felt deeply empowered once I had spoken in front of this group. *I didn't think I could do that, but I did*, I realized. *What else can I do?* Each month, I took on a new challenge. Sometimes I just had fun and experimented, but other times I developed skills or met people who helped me along my path to purpose. All of it was an investment in myself, and each challenge built my confidence in myself and what I was capable of, even if the results weren't measurable. Through this, I learned a lot about following the little urges that came to me without questioning them.

Acceptance, trust, and surrender are called for as your soul guides you where you're meant to go. You will notice that a profound sense of serenity surrounds you and that the connection you now have to your soul brings with it a purifying, calming, and restorative energy. Rather than having to be intentional about rest and relaxation as you were not so long ago, it has become your natural state, even with all of this forward movement.

You can now make what once felt impossible possible. You're living your life according to your interests rather than someone else's expectations or ideas of success. You are experiencing excitement and joy as part of daily life, and rigor and discipline don't feel taxing because they're directed toward your purpose and fueled by divine guidance. You can feel and experience the beauty you hold within, and you have a deep understanding of your connection to the direct energy of God, and know that you are never alone—and, for that matter, never were.

All of this eliminates the fears that have been embedded in your human experience up to this point, because you now exist in a flow of loving energy. You want to experience and deeply feel this journey you're on in all of its splendor and detail. It's as if each of your senses have been awakened and enlivened in a way you never knew was possible up to this point. For as much as you may have stumbled and felt tossed around before, here you are on a path of grace, joy, and inner peace. Your path *wants* you to walk it, and you can feel that, almost as if you're being magnetized forward.

With your freshly discovered sense of quiet, you can hear your soul's voice for entire moments at a time now and bring what it's telling you into your daily life, into the world where you can manifest your soul's desires. If all of this sounds magical, that's because it is. This part of the labyrinth is just as much a portal as a path. As you get closer to the center, you notice more and more synchronicities. These are signposts, guiding your way and confirming that you are on the right path. The path is now pulling you even as you walk it, closer and closer to your purpose. There's no going back—what once seemed so elusive is being drawn to you just as much as you're being drawn to it.

As you move toward your purpose and dreams, you also continue to move farther away from things that weren't meant for you or that held you back. You can see how all of the challenges and even the pain in your life were necessary to get you to this new place. With this comes so much compassion and love for your younger self, who didn't have the clarity you have now.

Walking the Path of the Legs

When I think about the importance of action when it comes to purpose, the movie *Charlie and the Chocolate Factory* comes to mind. There's a scene at the beginning of the movie when Charlie's older family members are all lying in bed, sick and weak. It seems like they're just waiting for something to happen to them, whether it's death or some miraculous force to present itself and make their lives better. Meanwhile, precious time is passing. I see this in real life too, as if people are just waiting on others or on time itself to somehow magically get them where they want to be. That's the big lesson in this chapter: the time for waiting ends now. An entire life can be wasted waiting for the golden ticket to arrive. Now you know where you need to go, and you have this magical connection with the universe and your guides and angels who have been waiting for this opportunity to work together to change the trajectory of your life.

No matter how much energy you've cleared and freed and how much spiritual support you've connected with, realizing your dreams will require bold steps—and that's exactly what you're doing on this path of the labyrinth. Whereas there may have been points in your life when others took the lead, now you are taking full responsibility. You *want* to take the lead and can feel yourself moving with confidence toward this clear vision and dream.

You are responsible for taking these leaps that will drive you forward, yes, but an otherworldly force will also flow through you. In the biography *Martha: The Life and Work of Martha Graham*, the renowned dancer and choreographer is quoted as explaining that a vitality and specific sort of life force energy quickens us and is translated through the desire—the *need*, even—to take action in a certain direction:

> There is a vitality, a life force, an energy, a quickening that is translated through you into action, and because there is only one of you in all of time, this expression is unique. And if you block it, it will never exist through any other medium and it will be lost. The world will not have it. It is not your business to determine how good it is nor how valuable nor how it compares with other expression. It is your business to keep it yours clearly and directly, to keep the channel open.

It's not up to us to determine how valuable that action seems or how it compares with the ways in which others are taking action to move forward in their own lives. This quickening action is a unique signature; if you don't bring it into the world, no one else can, because it is meant solely and specifically for you. This is why it's so vital to remain open to and aware of the urges that motivate you. The kind of action these urges inspire won't feel frenetic, but purposeful. If you find yourself feeling frantic or lost, it's a signal to regather your power and focus and reattune to hear where your path is calling you and what it's beckoning you to do. It's through this action that you will break free and realize your bigger purpose in life. It's how your soul's desire is expressed and birthed from your inner world into the outer world, and you are quite literally the only person who can bring this vision into the world. If you're looking for clarity, ask God, *Where do you want me to go today? Who needs a message from me or who do I need a message from to help me move in the right direction?*

If you're like many of my clients, this might feel new to you. Many of the women I work with are (or, more accurately, once were) what I like to call the Silent Wife. No matter how accomplished they are, there's a deference to them and even the actions they're aching to take are pushed aside in favor of what those around them expect (or pressed down so far that it reaches a point where their dreams can't even be accessed). I assume these women find me because I *was* that woman before I began getting quiet myself.

The way out of this deference is through confident action. There is so much power and strength available to you on this path that's beckoning you forward, so much life force. Your legs move your dreams forward, building more and more strength as they go. You can see and feel this expansion moving your life in a direction that feels in perfect alignment with the deepest, truest part of yourself. You feel better, happier, more excited, and more at peace with each step you take in this direction, which only serves to power you farther and farther along this path, constantly gaining momentum and a better view of what's ahead. For the first time in a long time, you can see and feel that you are making progress, and progress generates more excitement, more happiness, and less deference.

Whereas life before may have felt draining, now those legs of yours want to jump out of bed in the morning, powered by the enthusiasm and excitement you have not just for life but for your *specific* life. There's almost an urgency to this feeling that you must keep moving, and you can feel the buzz of the energy of life itself coursing through and swirling around you.

The action that you're taking now has a leader energy to it. You are not being led by another person, but by yourself and your desires, confident in your inner guidance, fully engaged and aware along each step of the path. With each step you take, you are confident in your value and comfortable in your own skin, because you're living out the expression of your true nature. Sometimes the action necessary might not look how you might imagine. It might not make perfect sense to you in the moment, or it could simply be creating and maintaining the space you need to continue to nurture and hold tight to your own dreams. For example, I worked with a client named Joanna, who was a high school history teacher, which meant she had summers off. Every year, she used this time to travel internationally. To the outside world, there seemed to be no rhyme or reason to the places she visited. They weren't hot spots or typical vacation destinations but, instead, places where she felt called and that were usually off the beaten path. On these adventures, she moved as slowly as possible, speaking with whomever and doing whatever she felt called to, doing things that made her feel healthy and alive, like learning new medicinal recipes from different cultures and partaking in local healing modalities. She wanted to learn new things so that she could take them home with her and continue to nourish herself in ways that helped her feel most like herself, that kept the fire in her belly burning. Initially, there wasn't a direct line between Joanna's travels and her purpose, but these adventures fueled her and were an important part of nourishing herself. After many years of doing this, Joanna realized that her mission was to shed light on the unique healers she encountered around the world, and she became a health tour guide for others who wanted to explore their health and wellness in alternative ways. Her teaching skills also came in handy for sharing the benefits of the practices they were engaging in with the travelers in her group, since most of the healers didn't speak English. Joanna took a circuitous route to her purpose, but never once did she question her dreams. She embraced and acknowledged them and took action long before she understood where those actions were leading her.

Other times, action may be no more than a word to create the space you need to keep moving along the right path: a simple yes to what you want or a no to what doesn't feel good to you. Those answers will come easier to you now—instantaneously, really—even if they don't always make logical sense. Remember, we're out of the logical mind and functioning from a much deeper, all-knowing place. There was a point in my coaching and speaking career when a well-known teacher in the self-help and spiritual space invited me to join her team. At an earlier time, I would have leapt at this invitation, because I was still lost and didn't yet understand my own direction. But when the offer came, I took the decision to the labyrinth and heard a clear *no* ring throughout my body, despite the fact that the offer was indisputably excellent on paper—an obvious yes to anyone who was observing my situation from the outside looking in. When I took a holistic inventory of my life and what I envisioned for myself, I understood that the offer didn't align with my own purpose. From that point, a gracious no was easy. It left me feeling empowered and moved me along my own path feeling stronger than ever before. This has happened several times since then, and not once have I regretted a single no. It's almost as if each of these opportunities is a pop quiz and a chance for your soul to affirm your true north.

Visualization for the Legs

Find a comfortable seat, close your eyes, and connect to your Anywhere Breath. As you breathe, bring your focus to your legs. See yourself starting to walk with slow, intentional steps. As you take each step, focus on your knees leading the way, pulling you forward along the path of your life. Notice the strength of your thighs and how they easily propel you forward, one step at a time. As you visualize yourself walking, continue breathing intentionally. After several steps, see yourself coming to a stop.

Visualize gently lifting up each kneecap as if it were a lid on a bottle. With this lid lifted, you can see the stuck energy that has gathered here in your knees. Let it all flow out and drift away into thin air. When you sense the stuck energy has all been released, place the lid back on each kneecap and close it gently. With all of that energy released, notice the free-flowing energy in your lower extremities, strong and ready to move you in the direction your soul calls.

You're Almost There

Fear can set in at this point. You might begin to think about all the things that could go wrong, because your life has moved forward in such significant ways and you're so far from where you began. What if you're in deeper than you're ready for? It might feel like this, but the reality is that you've just stepped onto a higher rung of the ladder and your ego is trying to protect you. Should you experience this, the most important thing is to keep going. You can think of it as a person falling off a building: it's not the falling that kills them, it's the stopping. You've worked so hard to generate this momentum—keep it going. Stay focused on taking even small actions in those moments when you might feel fearful of moving forward, because stopping abruptly can kill a dream.

If you find yourself experiencing these fears, remember that your dream will never lead you astray, even if it requires you to take action and make adjustments that will alter your life in significant ways. Remember that the direction you're feeling called to in this moment is leading you to the truest and most realized version of yourself, and nothing feels better than that.

Connect with the sense of joy and celebration in the air because you've come all this way. Your guides and angels take you by the hand and dance right alongside you as you approach the final path that will lead you toward the center of the labyrinth.

YOU ARE NOW CONNECTED

TO AND CHANNELING THE

POWER THAT HAS ALWAYS

EXISTED WITHIN YOU,

JUST WAITING TO BE

UNLEASHED AND BROUGHT

INTO THE WORLD.

CHAPTER NINE

GET INSPIRED

Follow Your Soul's Lead

Intuition is the language of silence, the existential language. The word in-tuition means to listen within yourself. Intuition is the silent voice within, which is already in contact with existence. Intuition is the voice of God.

— SWAMI DHYAN GITEN, AUTHOR AND SPIRITUAL TEACHER

Walking the Labyrinth

Open your intuition.

As you near the end of your journey, you step onto path 5, associated with your tailbone. You are feeling inspired and lit up. Because your system is so clear, you are able to easily channel information, almost as if a radio signal were originating from the base of your tailbone and traveling all the way up your spine to your neck, bursting out of the top of your head and projecting your vision out across the canvas of all creation.

We are all intuitive; it's part of being human. As children, most of us are in touch with our natural state enough that we accept our intuition without question. But as life goes on, many of us disconnect from this innate ability for any number of reasons: because we're taught intuition isn't "real," because our life is too full of distractions, or because we don't trust either ourselves or the universe. Like many people, I was very in touch with my intuition as a child, but that connection faded as I grew older and began to look at the world through a less magical lens and felt more isolated and overwhelmed by my own experience. It was only as I walked farther down the Get Quiet path that my intuition returned once again—or at least I could access it again. When my intuition came back online, I knew that I was back in my power, returned to my natural state.

To be clear, it's not that my intuition left me (just as your intuition hasn't left you), but that I had lost my ability to recognize and hear it for many years. Ironically, it was during those years that I could have used my intuition the most. Instead, I let my overthinking mind drown out my intuitive voice, and as a result I acted from a place of fear and a feeling of limitation rather than a place of knowing and self-empowerment. I say all of this with grace and compassion, because I was doing the best I could at the time and certainly didn't realize how disconnected from my intuition I was. After all, I was regularly sitting in quiet contemplation, trying to create space for information to come through. The problem was that I hadn't yet consistently nurtured the quiet, fertile ground that would allow me to actually hear my intuition over the clattering of my thoughts. Despite the fact that I couldn't hear my intuition even as it flowed through me, I now understand that it was always there. Intuition is like a wise old woman who always walks beside you, whether you acknowledge her presence or not.

From the very first time I walked the labyrinth, I found that I received clear messages every time I rounded the bend to the center of the circle on this fifth path. At first I didn't understand that this path is directly related to intuition, but now that I do, it all makes sense.

Now that your purpose is clear, your intuition is activated to color in the details, arming you with profound powers to access what's available to you so that you can create it in the world. Here you find the details you need to know to bring your dreams into reality. Although we don't always think of it this way, inspiration and intuition go hand in hand. If you think of intuition as a match, inspiration is the flame that bursts forth once it's struck, providing the light that will help you continue forward. Suddenly, you can access this instantaneous, powerful, and inspiring knowing of what's ahead to propel yourself forward toward the life of purpose that's waiting for you. This is powerful information you have access to and it's available because you are now connected to and channeling the power that has always existed within you, just waiting to be unleashed and brought into the world.

You have shed so much to get to this point. So much stress, so much noise, so much stuck energy, so many of the perceived limitations that were claiming your energy before. With all of this weight lifted and shifted, and all of this stress and pressure alleviated, you are now primed to hear the clear messages that are pointing you along your life path toward what excites you the most. Once you understand your intuition, you will not only find that it communicates with you on a regular basis, but also that you are more easily able to trust what you hear and allow it to guide you in the right direction.

Your Constant Companion

Intuition is a superpower, and an endangered one in this busy world. Speaking to how we can no longer hear our own inner wisdom, author and monk Thomas Merton wrote that "The rush and pressure of modern life are a form, perhaps the most common form, of contemporary violence." You can think of intuition as a very literal form of life support that touches every area of your life in every way imaginable. An intuitive signal is always there, guiding you toward every good decision available to you and warning you away from those that don't serve you. Your intuition understands information before you can intellectually process it, because it senses energy ready to become form. At its core, intuition is the ability to understand something immediately, without the need for conscious logic or reasoning. It allows you to tap into the superhighway of information that is flowing above and around you every second of every day, whether you recognize its existence or not. There's nothing you have to do or believe in for this intuition to exist—it just *is*, no different than the blood that constantly runs through your veins, keeping you alive. You don't have to think about this essential function for it to exist, it's just there, supporting your humanity. What *is* up to you is whether or not you acknowledge and intentionally connect with and embrace that intuition.

Ignoring our intuition often results in a sense of feeling lost. When intuition emerges and is acknowledged, we feel whole, like nothing is missing either within ourselves, in our life, or in the universe. Whereas before you likely felt a sense of unshakable frustration as the result of your intuition nudging you that something was missing from your life, now there's a sense of firing on all cylinders and having the support and guidance you need to get where you're trying to go. Maybe you could sense your intuition before but didn't have the trust in either the universe or yourself to listen and act upon it in the way intuition requires. Or perhaps you understood exactly what was happening, yet still deferred to the world of logic, just as we are all taught to do in the modern era of the Western world.

Through channeling with my guides, I've learned that intuition comes to us from a combination of energies, including guides, angels, and the infinite; the information intuition has to offer is disbursed to us through "the field." Each of us has a unique field that is created by our infinite energy. It's in this field that intuition comes through as a picture, a thought, or a knowing. Intuition can also speak through "coincidences" and other messages that find you at just the right moment. All of these forms and manifestations are your intuition staying connected to you and lighting your path. The more expansive and high-vibrational your energy field is, the more you can connect with and elevate to higher states of consciousness here on earth. Although each of our fields is unique and we each access it in our own way, the ultimate intent of the intuition that comes through the field is for the greater good. Even with that understanding, intuition is elusive and difficult to define or explain. Really, intuition has to be felt and experienced to be understood.

Whether you're a believer or not, stories about intuition run rampant, and you've likely experienced it at work either in your own life or the lives of others. You might have heard stories about a person who was supposed to be on a plane that crashed or who randomly ended up in the right place at the right time to meet their future spouse. And, yes, it's likely that a lot of people who have intuitive hits like this haven't done the work you've done to arrive at this place of quiet, but they can still access their intuition. That's because the messages are always there, regardless of the state we're in. Sometimes the desire or deep understanding that we *must* hear them is powerful and profound enough that intuition is able to break through the noise.

I have a brilliant and brave friend named Laura Penhaul, who navigated a rowboat nine thousand nautical miles across the Pacific Ocean from California to Australia with three other women. They were unassisted on their nine-month journey, and their trip was ultimately shared in a documentary called *Losing Sight of Shore*. For much of the trip, there were no other boats in sight, just these four women in the middle of the ocean for months on end trying to survive. The feat was so great that they weren't breaking a record but *establishing* one, quite literally doing something that no one had accomplished up to that point. From the moment she first heard about the voyage, Laura knew that it was something she was meant to take part in—despite the fact that she'd never rowed before. She explains, "I wanted something that was a blank canvas to me, something completely unknown so that I could test and challenge myself in seeing whether an open mind and ability to adapt and learn could make it possible to go from never having rowed before to rowing the largest ocean in the world." Not everyone in Laura's life agreed that this was a good decision, but when she was faced with challenge or doubt, she tuned in to herself and understood that, at some point in her lifetime, someone would make this first voyage of its kind, so why not her?

In the moments when intuition came into play throughout the expedition, she told me, "The feel was always visceral. It wasn't just a thought; it was a belief that impacted every cell in my body. It was a feeling of reaching forward to achieve, to adapt, to learn and grow on the go, that this was mine to achieve and only I could drive it." The impact of this was huge. "It gave me confidence, it gave me a sense that there was something bigger than me to achieve this for, but also a spiritual feeling that was bigger than the self. I wouldn't go so far as to say it made me feel invincible, but it definitely gave me the confidence not to give up, because there was something behind me, supporting me, always there going shoulder to shoulder with me."

As Laura experienced, intuition is here to be a partner, collaborator, and guiding force as you live your daily life and work toward creating your soul's legacy. Just like any partner, the more time you spend with your intuition and the more experiences you have with it, the more you will integrate intuition into your life and learn to trust and rely on it. Ultimately, you will come to see intuition for what it is: your endlessly loyal life companion.

Walking the Path of the Tailbone

Intuition is fun and affirming, but it can also be difficult, because it's usually such a subtle energy. It's sort of like if a parent silently enters your bedroom, leaves a sweet treat on the nightstand, then walks back out. The placement of the intuitive information is so quiet that you don't even notice it happening. Nonetheless, the information is there and it's beautiful, even if you didn't notice its arrival. In other words, even at the point when you're quiet and tuned in, you still have to play with your intuition and figure out how it works. It's not as simple as being given a process and then putting that process into practice, because each of us has a unique energy field and a unique set of angels and guides who will communicate in their own specific manner. Not only that, but we each receive that information in our own unique way.

Rather than letting this intimidate you, relax into each intuitive moment, because that's exactly the kind of energy that intuition thrives on. As soon as you take intuition too seriously, you will inadvertently block yourself. You might try asking your intuition simple questions, like: *Should I turn left here or right? Where do you want me to go today? Is there anyone in this room I should talk to?* Or you might try journaling when you're seeking guidance or insight. Journaling can serve both as a way to empty yourself and create a clear vessel, and as a way of creating an opening for the guidance and collaboration of the universe to come through you. In this space, a Godflash—a moment of sudden clarity and intense connection to divine energy—can enter, and your soul can speak.

When you receive an intuitive hit, write it down so that you're capturing the guidance as closely to how it came in as possible. In addition to keeping a record of the times and ways your intuition has come through, by writing down the guidance it has to share, you're making the information a real, solid thing, further absorbing and reinforcing its wisdom, and respecting the source the information originated from.

Notice and track what happens when you follow direction. This is how you build up confidence and familiarity with your intuition and understand how you can best open up to and work with it. I also encourage you to connect with a friend or small group of like-minded people so that you don't feel alone with your experience of intuition. When we support one another in this endeavor and see how universal and available intuition is and the things it's capable of, it strengthens our own understanding of intuition and supports a different way of living. The impact of this is immeasurable and can be a catalyst for families, communities, and ultimately, the entire planet to become happier, healthier, and more connected and empowered.

As you play with your intuition, there will also likely be times when you feel as if it's leading you astray. There's information to be gleaned here, too, and lots of room for curiosity. While I understand the temptation to question your intuition, more important is questioning the process through which you came to the insight that you believe your intuition provided. Know that if a voice is ever forceful or fear-based, it's not your intuition. Also understand that intuition can't be forced (though you can—and should!—request its guidance as you wish). Intuition is gentle and matter of fact; it arrives gracefully, as if it's being gently placed within your awareness. Your ego, on the other hand, speaks loudly, forcefully, and frequently. The information it provides is often disorganized, as opposed to the simplicity of intuitive information. Another way of differentiating between the two is noticing whether the guidance being provided is leading you toward a life of stress, poor health, or settling, as opposed to leading you toward your passion and impact and ultimately your greatness. This is because the ego speaks to your lower vibrational needs while your intuition is always seeking to guide you to a higher vibrational state.

The presence that you've cultivated up to this point and that you can continue to practice on a moment-to-moment basis creates a fertile ground for intuition and allows you to recognize and capture it when it comes. Getting yourself into a flow state is also important for intuition. One of my favorite experiences is when a client and I sync with one another in such a way that my intuition starts flowing through, almost as if I'm simultaneously listening to my client and my intuition, with those two streams of information being processed simultaneously, like they're dancing together and merging to bring in the most helpful and clear answers. Not only are we deeply present in moments of flow, but there's also a purity to them, where our heart and intentions are aligned with the highest good for all. Whenever we are acting for the highest good or helping our fellow human beings, it's like a fast track for intuition. The universe is always ready to help when a person enters this state of being. Pay attention and you can actually feel the click when the universe pops in to support your intentions;

it's a deeply satisfying, sometimes even ecstatic experience. It's in these moments that I often also find myself feeling acutely aware of how vital and sacred this quiet I've sowed in my life really is, and there's no doubt that it's worth every single moment of the challenges and pain that might have come from the processing required of us earlier in the labyrinth.

In its highest form, intuition is nothing short of magical. As it pulsates up and down your spine at the speed of light, drawing information from your energy field into your consciousness, it can even put you in direct communication with what can't be seen. For some, this is an innate ability, but for others it develops over time as the universe sees that you believe, as if you've done the work to build a solid and stable bridge that allows you to have one foot planted on earth and the other in the heavenly realm. Your intuition connects you to both of those places, and the degree and quality of information you can channel from this place is astounding and, quite literally, otherworldly. Once you're here, you live life in a completely different way than those around you who are still living in the noise of the world, disconnected from all of the very real energies around all of us. Your life will begin to feel extraordinary and everything you do will feel right. The answers you seek will be at your fingertips, and you will generally feel far less suffering because of this understanding of connection. Things that once weighed heavily upon you will feel much lighter and will no longer linger in your energy field or remain unresolved in your heart, because you have such a depth of understanding, safety, and security.

Finally, it's important to understand that even when you reach the point where you are living into your intuition, it doesn't necessarily mean that the people in your life will understand, and that can feel difficult—almost as if you've painted a beautiful masterpiece and then someone comes along and spray-paints all over it. The truth of the matter is that sometimes other people won't understand your commitment to your intuition or even acknowledge it as a power that exists. When this happens it can sometimes feel difficult not to be swayed, particularly if the feedback comes from someone whom you love or respect. In these moments, know that walking your own path and following your intuition will only make your connection with it stronger. Your intuition and your journey with it are for you alone, and with each collaboration you engage in, the stronger and more undeniable the connection between you and your intuition will be—whether others recognize that or not.

Visualization for the Tailbone

Because we spend so much time sitting, the tailbone energy is blocked in 100 percent of people. So that this channel is as open and free-flowing as possible, lie on your belly with your tailbone toward the sky. Visualize a soft breeze sweeping over and rustling your tailbone, as if gently waking it up, softly shaking the dense, stuck energy free. The breeze picks up some momentum and swoops over your tailbone, clearing away old lifetimes of pain and the hardships of this life. Then, with a final gust, it sweeps the area clean, whipping the formerly stuck energy away with it.

Intuition as Inspiration

When I first started my coaching practice and it began to grow quickly, I should have been delighted; in many ways, I was. I knew that I had found my purpose to facilitate healing, but what I believed to be true about both my own healing and that of others seemed out of step with what society in general had to say about healing. I wanted to understand more about how the mind, body, and soul worked together to create a joyful, healthy life, and yet no matter where I looked, what I read or researched, I couldn't find an answer that resonated with me. I knew there was more to healing than I understood and I wanted a deeper grasp of it for both myself and others; I was sure there was another level to healing that I couldn't quite access. But I was also scared—scared that I wasn't smart enough, good enough, or capable enough. Scared that what I believed and what I was doing didn't look like what everyone else was doing. I worried that I didn't *really* have the capacity for coaching and that clients would figure this out or, even worse, that I would somehow lead them astray. There was this sense that I'd gotten in over my head.

I could hear intuition pushing me forward, telling me to go in 100 percent, and yet I felt myself retreating. In fact, I was literally on a retreat in Central Mexico, trying to find space to sit with all of this so that the answers could rise to the surface, when I found myself driving off to a remote area alone in a car with a driver who I had never met before and who spoke a different language. Did I mention I was asked to leave my cell phone behind? This is something that my logical mind would *never* allow me to do, and yet I couldn't shake this inner guidance, which was telling me that I needed to take this trip to meet with a shaman, Enrique, and his wife, Sabrina, who was also a healer. Despite all of my confusion, I could also feel that a door was opening for me and that something new and exciting was on the other side, but I wasn't quite sure what that was. I just knew I had to access it. And I knew that, somehow, this meeting with Enrique and Sabrina was part of getting to that other side.

After two and a half hours of driving through unfamiliar terrain, the vehicle finally slowed and rattled to a stop on a dirt road, where I saw a couple of unassuming structures that blended into the land. A few dogs danced around at the heels of the man who approached the car. As I stepped out, I couldn't help but notice that everything felt . . . healthy. The *land* felt healthy, as did the dogs, the birds, the trees, and the smiling man who was now standing in front of me. Enrique was in his 60s, with leathery skin and lines crisscrossing his face, but I could feel the vitality rolling off him. I could also feel that he was a person on a sacred mission—his energy wasn't at all forceful, but it was intense. All of the fears I'd had on the drive here immediately disappeared. I knew I was safe and exactly where I was meant to be.

Enrique walked me inside one of the earth-colored buildings and into an inviting, brightly tiled kitchen, where Sabrina was waiting with a green juice that tasted so fresh and alive, it was as if my taste buds had sprung to life and stood at attention. While Enrique talked and explained what I could expect over the next couple of days, Sabrina listened, clearly soaking me in.

The next day, Enrique and I slowly walked the rolling hills of the land under the hot August sun. We stopped frequently, as he showed me different plants and herbs and demonstrated what the various flowers, leaves, and berries could be used for. It was like a master class in nature, how the natural environment mingles with and heals our human nature, plant medicine, and sustainability. When Enrique and I weren't talking, the silence between us was filled with the sound of a running stream, birds singing, and unseen animals scampering across our path. It was as if I was breathing in the environment, the energy of the land, and all of the information that Enrique shared with me. Finally, we came to a clearing in the dense trees where we could look out and survey the valley beneath us. He turned to me and said, "You are a bridge from modern medicine to holistic. The beautiful, peaceful smile on your face will make them want what you have."

I was speechless. I hadn't actually told Enrique why I had come to see him and Sabrina or the information that I had been reaching for but not quite able to grasp. I felt seen and validated. And here in nature, I remembered how much I had missed it. I'd spent my childhood surrounded by the grand redwood forests of Northern California, and then gradually became more and more disconnected from it as an adult. In that moment I understood that I'd spent all of this time seeking answers, when really they were all inside. I realized that I could do what Enrique did, and that, in fact, it's what I'd already been doing—and that it was enough. Rather than seeking and working so hard to find answers for the people I worked with, I could simply support them in just *being* in a quiet space where they could tune in to their nature and remember who they were and that all of the answers are already inside.

I came off the mountaintop a couple of days later with the answers that I hadn't expected but needed. I understood that I felt sick, we all feel sick, because we're so disconnected from our natural state. No medicine is going to heal that. It's only by returning to this natural state that we can feel restored and remember who we are and why we're here.

And that's how intuition works. Sometimes the answers are clear and specific. Other times intuition nudges you, letting you know where to go next, whose path you're meant to cross, even if it doesn't make any sense. Intuition places you in a space where you can find the inspiration you need to remember your own answers and to keep moving forward from there. But when you press down your ability to intuit—as so many of us do, often without even realizing it—you suffer as a result, and you also miss out on the deepest expression of yourself. Not to mention the fact that the world does too.

All of that ends now as you connect with this energy emanating up from your tailbone and the vision it brings up from there. When you trust in your power and ability to intuit, you have that final piece of the puzzle to transform your dreams into reality through glimpses of the various puzzle pieces that are lying there right in front of you, just waiting to be put together. Trust that you've already come so far from where you started and now it's just a matter of assembling the details, which your intuition is eagerly waiting to illuminate for you. Once you lean in, this intuition will ignite the inspiration that leads to and confirms your deeper knowing.

Keep trusting long enough for your dreams to become reality. Once you can do this, once you can give yourself evidence that your intuition *is* reliable and it *is* guiding you along the unique path you're meant to walk, it's like a full graduation into your intuition.

You have done the hard work to know that you are powerful and can trust yourself and now you can breathe and relax into that. You can trust your dreams, develop your intuition, and allow inspiration to flow through you. Once you experience your intuition and what it feels like to live an awakened life, you will come to realize you can trust it more than any other experience you once deemed "more real." And in those moments when you *do* lose sight of your intuition, know that it's always there, waiting patiently for you to connect with it again.

YOU WILL NEVER GET LOST

AGAIN OR LOSE FOCUS

ON YOUR PURPOSE OR

INSPIRATION. THERE IS

NO GOING BACK FROM

HERE BECAUSE YOU'VE

FOUND THE CENTER

PLACE OF YOU.

CHAPTER TEN

GET CONNECTED

Stand in Wholeness

*There is one unity, unified wholeness, total natural law,
in the transcendental unified consciousness.*

— MAHARISHI MAHESH YOGI, FOUNDER OF THE
TRANSCENDENTAL MEDITATION MOVEMENT

Walking the Labyrinth

*Realize your connection with the soul, feel your energy exchange
with the heavens, and live from this place every day.*

In the center of the labyrinth, associated with the shoulders,
there is no more path to walk. Instead, there is stillness at long last
as your soul greets your body and they become one, fully merged.
Rays of light shine out of your shoulders and rise up to the heavens
to meet unity consciousness. You now stand in your wholeness, both
divine and human.

Here at the center of the labyrinth, your body and soul converge. No wonder your sense of direction has been increasingly clear—it has been your soul calling out for you all along, leading you closer and closer back to it. Now that they have reunited, there is a profound sense of homecoming, a feeling of belonging to yourself, and an indescribable sense of peace and fulfillment. You have merged together these two halves of a divine masterpiece and their reunion is the ultimate act of self-love and self-realization. It's here in this sacred union that you discover the true essence of your humanity, which transcends the limitations of the physical world and embraces the infinite potential within you.

You feel an immense sense of wholeness, like you've found the most important missing piece of yourself—because you have. Now that you've connected with your soul, it makes sense why you've felt lost and perhaps even lonely for so long. *This* is what it means to fall in love with yourself. That rush of euphoria and excitement that you've felt before when you've fallen madly in love is now available to you at every moment of every day and is dependent upon no one other than yourself. That beautiful free-flowing energy of love will overflow into everything you do and every person you encounter, just like love does. Now that the body and soul have found one another, you leave the labyrinth together to walk back into the world hand in hand. This entire journey has been for one purpose: to return to love. And to remember that all the love you ever needed was inside of you all along.

When you feel this kind of love, you become a magnet, pulling all forms of pure love toward you as well as all of the goodness and kindness that comes with it. You realize that to have the love you want, all you have to do is to *be* the love you want. What you are really experiencing here is unity consciousness, a higher state of awareness that recognizes the oneness of all existence. Whereas you started this journey feeling lost, confused, and disconnected, you have now transcended to a state where you have a cellular understanding of your interconnectedness with the universe, the divine, and others on this human plane. It's impossible to feel this without also experiencing a deep sense of love, compassion, and harmony, which dissolve any barriers or divisions you previously perceived. It is this unity consciousness flowing through you that leads to profound peace and joy.

Two beams of light rise up from the top of your shoulders to the heavens as the light of the infinite shines back down on you from the heavens, creating a swirl of radiant, true love that comes from the most vast and powerful level of consciousness. You are one with that well of light and love now, ready to draw it forth and bring it into the world. You are matching the vibration of life and creation itself. You are home.

Standing in the Center

The journey to the center of the labyrinth has been long, but worth it. Most of us have not yet consciously connected with our soul in this lifetime, so this opportunity to do so is precious. As you take a deep breath and stand here surveying the paths you've traveled to get to this point, a range of emotions washes over you. It's exciting and there's also a comfortable intimacy to it that allows you to experience complete security and wholeness in your own company. It feels so *right* and natural that you wonder how it is you haven't felt this all along.

There is a dichotomy here because really, what you've done is to reconnect with your own soul and inner being, returning to your truest self. And yet it feels so novel and is such a new experience because in this human experience we're all about connecting to the outer world rather than the inner one. It is a return to how we were meant to live: energetically aligned and connected to ourselves and the world. It feels sacred here in the center and also very human because it is the place where the soul and human merge together into perfect harmony. You've heard the saying before that you are a soul having a human experience, but here you really *feel* and understand that. Now that you've felt this whole, united version of yourself, you will never get lost again or lose focus on your purpose or inspiration. There is no going back from here because you've found the center place of *you*, where your body and soul converge.

Here in the center where this unity consciousness dwells, we revel in a kind of love and compassion that most of us have never experienced before. On the 3D plane, there is no such thing as truly unconditional love; even if someone loves you *almost* unconditionally, it's still not the same because the ego is always present. This love here in the center isn't tethered by any conditions; it is truly limitless and unconditional because it comes from beyond humanity. Now that you feel this kind of unwavering support, you realize that you never lost your power at all, even when you couldn't feel it—it's been there, just waiting for you to reunite with it.

While so many things in this world feel impermanent, you understand that no one can ever take the work that you've done to get to this point away from you. Along the way you've not only learned so much, but you've acquired all of these new tools and perspectives in the process. Each and every path you've walked to get to this point is deeply and vitally important. You now know how to quiet your mind and your body so that you can hear your soul's voice. You know how to access all of the guidance, support, and information that are your birthright. You know how to hear what really matters. The voice of your soul now vibrates throughout every cell of your body and molecule of your being, and there's no way that it could ever be mistaken for the chatter of the overthinking mind. That would be like mistaking a whisper for a roar.

When people say the world has gone crazy, it's because they've only connected to their body and mind, not their soul. Once you remember and experience this alignment, not only will you realize how beautiful and perfectly designed you are, but also that the world is a beautiful, kind, and generous place. You find yourself joyful, filled with love for it all. It matters to you and your life path that you find this unity, and it also matters immensely to everyone in your life and to the world at large. The more people who reconnect body and soul, the more likely that this entire planet and all of the beings who live here will rediscover our true nature and expand our consciousness. Unification with the self ultimately blossoms into the unification of the world. Of all the problems in the world today, the biggest and most dire is that we have separated our body from our soul and don't understand that they are constantly in communion with one another. To live as we are meant to, we must understand that we are equally human and divine, equally of earth and of heaven. Now you have been reminded of that connection and have done the work to *feel* that connection on a profound level. It's as if the labyrinth is a launch-pad and the energy has gathered within you so that you can soar.

Visualization for the Shoulders

Sit down with your arms crossed across your chest and each hand gently placed atop the opposite shoulder. Notice the rise and fall of your chest as you take gentle and steady breaths. Visualize infinite rays of light flowing out of the tops of your shoulders and fanning up into the heavens. See the light connecting to everything everywhere. See this light gathering all of the love meant for you in this lifetime. Now watch the bright radiant love-filled light shine back down through your shoulders and infuse every cell in your body. Feel its warmth and healing energy from head to toe. Stay in stillness and soak in this state of bliss.

Walking the Path Back into the World

Just as important as walking into the labyrinth is walking back out of it. Once you've soaked up all of this beautiful, peaceful merging energy in the center of the labyrinth, you get to bring it back out into the world again. You will do that through your purpose, and you will also do it through your *being*, through your mere presence.

But before you do, pause here and feel those rays shining both out and up from your shoulders straight up into the heavens above and shining just as brightly down upon you, pouring into your shoulders. This light opens your shoulders up and back, which means that your heart space is now open so that infinite loving energy can flow in and out freely. Whereas you once felt lost and overwhelmed, you now understand that you not only feel but truly *are* powerful beyond measure. You possess the very real ability to light up the entire universe by inspiring others to heal themselves and live out their ultimate purpose, just as you are.

There are other people in the world just like you who are connecting to new energy fields of growth just as they are, bringing their purpose and dreams into reality on this planet you share. You can think of yourselves as little lights popping up across the earth, glowing brightly and steadily as you move around your path and about your life. No matter how big or small you feel, how physically far apart you are, you understand in the deepest sense that you are connected and working with these other bright lights to bring a new kind of healing to the planet.

As you move forward, remember that staying awake and attuned through both the beautiful and the challenging times ahead is the key to getting quiet and centered and to remaining whole, body, mind, and soul. Welcome it all into your life and know that you are ready for it. This *is* the human experience, and it is also the divine experience. Remember that you never have to be scared or shut down, because you were built for this. You were built to handle times of joy and times of sorrow, times of suffering, and times of prosperity. You've worked hard to get to this point and now all you have to do is remain here for it, in whatever the present moment brings. Surrender to each situation, each day, each moment, and know that you are supported as you move through it, always. Invite in the wisdom that is yours for the taking when you need it. Live life as it unfolds, meet life where it rises up to greet you, and don't resist what comes your way. Instead, breathe into it; stay awake and aware as it comes to you. Treat life as if it is a river, and you are there to meet its flow, allowing it to hold you through the natural twists and bends of the path your soul has imagined for you. Notice where you are at any moment in time, but don't exert the unnecessary energy of trying to look too far around the bend.

When you first embarked upon this path, your energy was waning, but now you are completely charged and lit up. You love yourself and life and are excited for the future. You know that you are a vital part of something so much bigger than you. Something that you are intricately connected to and that dwells within you. Along the way back to you, you have become accustomed to talking to God, who has walked with you this entire way. Keep that conversation going because He is always there to guide you through every step you take. Remember that this guidance is always there, even when the noise of the world tries to drown it out.

Embrace the loving light that shines down upon you in the center of the labyrinth, and feel it continue to shine upon you as you retrace your steps back out of the labyrinth and into the world. Feel it as you make your way back to the outside world, forever changed and bringing with you all that you have learned. Because it's there outside the labyrinth, living this human experience of yours, where you will live out your soul's legacy, whole and undeterred by the noise of the world.

CONCLUSION
Living a Quiet Life

While the path you've just walked will transform your life, know that getting quiet is a journey that you will intentionally embark on again and again throughout your life, rather than a one-time solution. Sometimes you may fall off of the path, and when that happens, it's okay!

When your world starts to get noisy or it becomes hard to feel your connection to that still, small voice or to hear your intuition, understand that these are simply reminders for you to tune back in again. What's important is that now you've cultivated the awareness to understand when this disruption is occurring. In these moments, you may feel called to walk the entire sequence of the labyrinth again and to holistically quiet yourself one path at a time. Or it may be just one area of yourself or your life that needs some attention. For example, maybe you've experienced a recent heartbreak and need to clean and clear your heart energy, or perhaps you've slipped on incorporating rest and relaxation into your life and need to focus specifically on clearing your hips to free up your flow of energy.

My deepest wish for you moving forward is to know you can heal yourself. There's a simple body scan you can do to identify where any stuck energy is in your body so that you can focus on that area to get your energy flowing once again. Doing this scan on a regular basis allows you to notice when energy is stagnant so that you can quickly move and heal it as necessary to keep your energy points in tune. This is very simple to do. Simply find a quiet space, connect with your breath, and focus on your energy points in the same order they appear in the labyrinth.

First, visualize sending your breath to your abdomen and notice how it feels. Do you sense any denseness or a blockage of flow? If you do, continue to breathe into that space and envision a healing ray of light beaming down from the sky and into that part of your body. Do this for as long as you feel called to, and if you sense that the energy point still needs more attention, return to that chapter and the practices discussed there. Repeat this same process along each energy point of the body, moving next to your heart, head, hips, feet, legs, tailbone, and shoulders. The more you practice scanning your energy like this and in this exact order, the more habitual and quicker the process will become. After a while, you may not even have to perform the scan anymore at all but will instead just *know* when a certain energy point is calling for some love and attention.

As you continue to follow the path of getting quiet, you'll find it gets easier and easier to tune in to your soul's voice. You may even discover you're able to open up to wisdom from a higher source. In fact, that's exactly what happened for me as I deepened my work with the Get Quiet Way in the years before writing this book. Following my own process led me to connect with a field of information beyond myself—beyond the physical plane—and to receive a powerful system for healing at the quantum level. I now practice this system, which I call the Nemus Code, with clients and also teach them to use it for self-healing. The good news for you is that you've already experienced the Nemus Code healing! It is based on the same eight energy points that have shaped our journey through the labyrinth together, the same points you tuned in to in the body scan I just described.

While this work is a lifelong process, it's so worth it—no matter when you start. I recently had the opportunity to speak with my dear friend Dorothy, a captivating woman with an understated elegance, a quick wit, and a deep love for life. She spoke to me about how finding quiet in her mid-90s changed her life. Up until that point, Dorothy kept allowing more and more noise into her world, which, she explains, pushed her further and further away from who she was. There was too much noise and not enough room to be still. It's never too late to change, though, and Dorothy did. When she talks about her journey to quiet, you can almost feel the gratitude emanating from her.

For most of her life, Dorothy was a busy and social person who was always in a hurry and who lived in an action- and reaction-seeking world. While she's still social and loves enjoying a sense of connection with both friends and strangers, today she's learned to balance this with making an intentional effort to quiet her life and herself. Now that she understands the importance of doing so, she's protective of the quiet she has cultivated. For example, Dorothy still loves to throw a party, but she's clear with her guests about when it's time to go. This is necessary, she says, because she now craves the quietness and needs to experience it on a daily basis.

Now that Dorothy has found quiet, she marvels at the richness and fullness to be found in every moment, at how satisfying this silence feels. Whereas she didn't slow down enough previously in life to feel like she owned her time, now Dorothy can "disappear into the clouds or the sun" or the big view of the ocean in front of her home in Maui. While quietly watching the beautiful palm tree in front of her window, Dorothy feels as if she connects to everything that crawls and grows. This connection fills her up and infuses her with confidence that now she can be a better, more thoughtful part of it all.

As you know by now, quiet isn't really quiet at all. It's the sound of your heart and soul, the sound of your inner knowing, the sound of the divine—and so much more. As Dorothy says, "It's the noises of the wind and it's the noises of the gardens, it's the noises of the sea."

Getting quiet allows us to hear what really matters.

DISCOVER MORE

To discover more go to elaineglass.net.

ACKNOWLEDGMENTS

To those who have loved and guided me: mostly my parents Don and Jeanne Glass, my patients, coaching clients, and countless spiritual teachers, thank you for helping me awaken to this beautiful life.

To Christina Rasmussen, I am truly grateful for your wisdom, love, and friendship. Without you, this book would not be possible.

To Anne Barthel, your keen editorial eye and gentle touch have brought soul to this project. With heartfelt gratitude, I thank you for your dedication and artistry.

To Nikki Van Noy, for your editorial and emotional genius. Everything good that is woven into these pages is because of your mastery. In my heart I thank you always.

To my love, Michael Fishman, for breathing life into me with your love, support, and unwavering commitment to helping me live out my dreams.

To Matthew and Mike, for being the spark of love, motivation, and inspiration for all I do. You are my greatest blessings.

Thank you to the magical town of Paradise Valley, Arizona, where this book began, and to the peaceful town of Prescott, Arizona, where it was completed.

To God and all of the divine forces that govern the Universe, for unconditional love and for shining a guiding light on my path.

To all who have come before me and all who will come after me, we join in a shared soul's calling: to contribute to the healing of the world. May this book serve as a beacon of light and inspiration, guiding others on their own spiritual path.

ABOUT THE AUTHOR

For more than a decade **Elaine Glass** has transformed lives with her healing presence and coached countless people to unlock their truest selves, finding purpose, peace, and self-empowerment.

At one point she found herself at a personal crossroads. A newly single mother, burned out, fearful, and alone, she lived the next decade in search of her own healing and inner truth.

She now travels the world sharing her holistic healing techniques, energy medicine methodologies, and spiritual guidance. Her mission today is to guide people in connecting with their soul's calling to bring lasting love, joy, and vitality.

Elaine resides in Paradise Valley, Arizona, across the street from her beloved labyrinth, where she welcomes people from around the world to her in-person retreats.

To discover more about Elaine Glass's community, newsletter, online courses, and in-person retreats, visit **www.elaineglass.net**.

We hope you enjoyed this Hay House book. If you'd like to receive our online catalog featuring additional information on Hay House books and products, or if you'd like to find out more about the Hay Foundation, please contact:

Hay House LLC, P.O. Box 5100, Carlsbad, CA 92018-5100
(760) 431-7695 or (800) 654-5126
(760) 431-6948 (fax) or (800) 650-5115 (fax)
www.hayhouse.com® • www.hayfoundation.org

———

Published in Australia by: Hay House Australia Pty. Ltd.,
18/36 Ralph St., Alexandria NSW 2015
Phone: 612-9669-4299 • *Fax:* 612-9669-4144
www.hayhouse.com.au

Published in the United Kingdom by: Hay House UK, Ltd.,
The Sixth Floor, Watson House, 54 Baker Street, London W1U 7BU
Phone: +44 (0)20 3927 7290 • *Fax:* +44 (0)20 3927 7291
www.hayhouse.co.uk

Published in India by: Hay House Publishers India,
Muskaan Complex, Plot No. 3, B-2, Vasant Kunj, New Delhi 110 070
Phone: 91-11-4176-1620 • *Fax:* 91-11-4176-1630
www.hayhouse.co.in

———

Access New Knowledge.
Anytime. Anywhere.

Learn and evolve at your own pace
with the world's leading experts.

www.hayhouseU.com